John Whitgift

Elizabeth I's last Archbishop of Canterbury

Christopher Barnett

*(Front cover) Detail
from a stained glass
window in Grimsby
Minster, portraying
Archbishop Whitgift*

ISBN 978-0-9517320-2-1

© The Whitgift Foundation 2015

Published by The Whitgift Foundation North End Croydon CR9 1SS

Contents

Acknowledgements

I would like to thank all those who have helped in various ways with the research, preparation and production of this book, in particular: the Governors of the Court of the Whitgift Foundation, for supporting this project; Graham Maudsley, for his creativity in designing the layout and setting the text, and his endless patience in completing the equally-endless changes; Beverly Gibson-Patteux and Bill Wood, for their help with sourcing the illustrations, and copyright approval; Felicity Hewson, for her general help, and for maintaining the steady flow of a vast quantity of sources, principally from the London Library, to which institution warm thanks are also due; Atiya Afghan, for assistance in effecting online access to a wide range of primary sources; Clara Barnett, Shirley Heath, Tates Lisoire, Sue Turnbull, Keith Smith and Matthew Lakin, who read and commented on the text before publication – any errors remaining would be of my own making; Sam Holland, who sculpted the wonderful bronze statue I commissioned for Whitgift School, in 2013, which features on page 115; Chris Marsh, for photography in Grimsby, Lincoln and Whitgift (pages 15-18, 40-41, 43, 105 and front cover), which is copyright of Whitgift School; Danny Fitzpatrick, for photography in Croydon (pages 86, 90, 108, 109, 115), which is copyright of Whitgift School; Mark Somerville, for the photography of Whitgift Foundation property (pages 7, 74, 87, 105, 111); Skypower, for the aerial photo of Whitgift School, which is copyright of Whitgift School (page 114).

I would especially like to pay tribute to the meticulous research undertaken by FHG Percy, particularly at Lambeth Palace Library, and in many other libraries and manuscript collections; a substantial amount of material remains in the Whitgift School Archive, which has informed and supported many of the judgments made in the pages which follow. I would also wish to acknowledge the importance of the vast array of secondary material produced by historians of the period. Those works which have been of most assistance, in assessing Whitgift and his times, are listed in the Select Bibliography, and are recommended for further reading.

Attempts have been made to contact relevant copyright holders, wherever possible; if any have been overlooked, this will be readily addressed for a subsequent edition, and apologies are expressed in advance. To enhance the readability of the text, all footnotes have been omitted, in line with a main aim of this study. Capital letters have generally been altered to lower case, in quotations from original sources, where they often appear in abundance. The location of a source quoted has, wherever possible, been included *in situ*. Where Whitgift's own words are cited, or those of his correspondents, they are readily searchable online, and most often to be found in the three volumes of Strype's *Life and Acts of John Whitgift*; in the three volumes of Ayre's *The Works of John Whitgift*; in Anderson's *Monuments and Antiquities of Croydon Church*; in Dr Ducarel's *Some Account of the Town of Croydon*; or in Raine's *Correspondence of Dr Matthew Hutton*.

Grateful thanks to the copyright owners for permission to publish are expressed to:

Grimsby Archives for the Wellow Abbey seal, p15; The Bodleian Library, University of Oxford, for MS Douce 276, f.10v, Schoolmaster and pupils, p19; The Master and Fellows of Trinity College, Cambridge, for Whitgift's coat of arms on Queen's Gate, p29; The Master and Fellows of Trinity College, Cambridge, for the portrait of John Whitgift, p32; National Portrait Gallery for the portrait of Thomas Cartwright, p33; The Master and Fellows of Peterhouse, Cambridge, for the portrait of John Whitgift, p30; Syndics of Cambridge University Library for Hammond's plan of Cambridge, dated 1592, Classmark: Atlas.2.92.1, p30; Great St Mary's, The University Church, Cambridge for the image of Great St Mary's, p31; Ely Cathedral photo library for the photo of Ely Cathedral, p42; Worcester Heritage and Amenity Trust for The Tudor Museum photo, p43; Worcester Cathedral, photo taken by Dr CA Barnett, pp44-45; National Trust for the photo of Greyfriars House, Worcester, p46; Worcester Cathedral for Whitgift's Register facsimile, p47; Trustees of Lambeth Palace Library for the Edward Blore watercolour, p56; Dean and Chapter, Canterbury, for Canterbury Cathedral photo, p56; National Portrait Gallery for portrait of William Cecil, 1st Baron Burghley, p57; Victoria and Albert Museum, London, for the mitre, dated circa 1592, p58; National Portrait Gallery for the portrait of Robert Devereux, 2nd Earl of Essex, p59; National Portrait Gallery for the portrait of Queen Elizabeth I, p70; National Portrait Gallery for the portrait of William Cecil, 1st Baron Burghley, p71; The British Library Board for Thomas Nashe's 'An Almond for a Parrat' 96.b.15(4) the title page, p72; Whitgift School Archives for the letter to John Whitgift's attorney, p73; Museum of Croydon for the letter from John Whitgift to John Boys, p73; Syndics of Cambridge University Library for John Speed's 'Theatre of the Whole Island of Great Britain' Surrey map, Classmark: Atlas.2.61.1, p74; National Portrait Gallery for the portrait of Richard Bancroft, p75; The British Library Board for Thomas Nashe's 'A pleasant Comedie, called Summers last will and Testament', C.34.d.50 title page, p88; National Portrait Gallery for the line engraving of Thomas Nashe, p89; Whitgift School Archives for the beechwood bowl photograph, p91; Whitgift School Archives for the Schoolmaster's House engraving, dated 1880, by CW Scott, p91; Whitgift School Archives for the Hospital of the Holy Trinity, Croydon, engraving by MJ Starling, Virtue & Co., 1881, pp92-93; National Portrait Gallery for the portrait of Queen Elizabeth I, p104; National Trust for the John Whitgift portrait at Knole House (John Whitgift (1530-1604), Archbishop of Canterbury, British (English) School, 1605/08 ©National Trust Images (The Sackville Collection), p107; Society of Antiquaries of London for the funeral procession of Queen Elizabeth I, drawn by William Camden, p106; Bridgman Art Library for John Whitgift's shoes, p106; Victoria and Albert Museum, London, for the photographs of the mazer bowls, on loan from the Whitgift Foundation, p110; The President of Surrey Archaeological Society for permission to make use of material from Marion Colthorpe's article, 'Queen Elizabeth I and the Croydon Horse Race' in Vol. 77 (published in 1986) of the Surrey Archaeological Society's Collections Journal; Cambridge University Press and The British Library Board for text extracts from Alastair Bellany, 'A Poem on the Archbishop's Hearse: Puritanism, Libel, and Sedition after the Hampton Court Conference', The Journal of British Studies, Volume 34(2), pp137-164, (1995), (The British Library reference: Add. 38139, f.58); Sutton Publishing, part of The History Press, for text extracts from 'The Mitre and the Crown' by Aidan Bellinger and Stella Fletcher, p103.

Preface

This biography examines the life, character and achievements of John Whitgift, the Elizabethan Archbishop. Despite the undoubted significance of Whitgift's impact on Church and State, no study of his life has been published for nearly fifty years. There has also been a tendency, on the part of historians, to caricature Whitgift, in the way that contemporary opponents did, in one-dimensional, negative fashion.

This book therefore has two principal aims: first, to make his life accessible and intelligible, in the light of current understanding of his times; and second, to demonstrate that his life was, in reality, a varied and fascinating one. Whitgift was not the narrow-minded bigot he has often been labelled, and was capable of showing more empathy for the opinions of others than many of his era.

Significant space has been allowed for Whitgift's own words, and for those of his first biographer, Sir George Paule, in particular. Paule served Whitgift as comptroller of his household, effectively his private secretary; his *Life of John Whitgift* was published in 1612, just under a decade after Whitgift's death. Paule's account is so full of admiration as to make it almost hagiographical, but it also has the immediacy and authority of an account based on detailed knowledge, and stories acquired from Whitgift at first hand. John Strype's extensive *Life and Acts of Archbishop John Whitgift*, published in 1822, is also strongly sympathetic.

Subsequent historical interpretation has, in general, been much less kind to Whitgift, concentrating heavily on seeing the Archbishop as a rather limited man, with tiresome, schoolmasterly tendencies, a man entirely consumed by his implacable opposition to the enemies of the Elizabethan religious settlement. Whitgift could indeed be a ruthless, and sometimes truly choleric, adversary. But he was capable of showing remarkable patience and surprising moderation, and he was highly intelligent and a gifted preacher. The importance of his contribution towards maintaining the stability of the Tudor state, in dangerous times, should not be underestimated.

The pages that follow will seek to demonstrate not only that Whitgift deserves credit for the achievement of his main goal, the preservation of the Elizabethan established Church, but also that he was an unusually complex man. His life and character are full of apparent contradictions: he was a passionate academic, yet one who could allow academia to be ridiculed; a chief censor, reviled by Shakespeare, in *Hamlet*, yet a lover of music and the arts, and warmly portrayed by Spenser, in the *Faerie Queene*; a ruthless adversary, yet a supportive friend and generous patron; a man who built up one of the finest of contemporary, private libraries, but who also had an interest in rural pursuits like hunting and fishing; and finally, a deeply-committed cleric, who gave a huge part of his life to the service of Church and State, yet whose private time, with his household in Croydon, was one of the most important aspects of his entire life.

Whitgift's commitment to education will also be shown to have been life-long. His beloved Foundation, his greatest legacy, still flourishes in Croydon. Whitgift's original School has been joined by two others, his Hospital by two additional care homes. Together they provide the wider social benefit to which Whitgift was committed when he established the Foundation, with such striking generosity, in the late 1590s.

Dr Christopher Barnett
Croydon, July 2015

The seal from the Letters Patent, of Queen Elizabeth I, November 1595, authorising Whitgift to commence his Foundation in Croydon

1

Early Life and Education – Great Grimsby, London and Cambridge

John Whitgift was born into a prosperous, Lincolnshire family, living in Grimsby, known then as Great Grimsby, to distinguish it from the smaller, nearby village of Little Grimsby. A commemorative plaque, on a later house at 37/39 Bethlehem Street, now marks the birthplace of the Archbishop. The Whitgift family had its roots in Yorkshire, less than fifty miles to the north-west of Great Grimsby, in the village of Whitgift; it is located on the River Ouse, to the west of its junction with the Trent, about five miles east of the town of Goole.

The exact date of John Whitgift's birth remains uncertain, occurring at some point between 1529 and 1534; it seems most likely to have been in 1530, the year recorded by his biographer, Sir George Paule. Formal registration of births in each parish was not required until 1538, but, while no document provides conclusive evidence, Whitgift himself stated, in 1590, that he was sixty years old. Whitgift's grandfather, John Whitgift of York, had one daughter, Isobel, and two sons, Robert, and Henry, the father of the Archbishop, who became a merchant in Great Grimsby, a fishing and trading port on the Humber estuary. Fishing remains important today, the Grimsby fish market being one of the most significant in Europe. The modern port would, however, be almost unrecognisable to the Whitgifts. It now services the offshore wind energy industry, and moves hundreds of thousands of cars each year. By the early sixteenth century, while the town remained locally significant, its national importance had been steadily declining, as the river had silted up through the previous century; at its high point, in the twelfth century, Great Grimsby ranked in the top dozen or so ports in England. The Church of St James, one of the finest in the region, recently re-named Grimsby Minster, remains to testify to the wealth and character of the old town. The Minster has stained glass windows portraying John Whitgift, one showing him kneeling at the death-bed of Queen Elizabeth I.

Henry Whitgift prospered from his investments in the sea-borne trade, and owned a number of houses in the town, where he also held office, becoming an Alderman in 1550; he married Anne Dynewell, who was born in Great Grimsby. Following a not uncommon practice, he gave his own father's name, John, to his eldest son, the future Archbishop, who was to be one of seven children, his siblings being his brothers William, George, Philip, Richard and Jeffrey, and sister, Alice. FHG Percy, who researched the family history, found no trace of surviving nephews and nieces beyond the two sons and four daughters born to Whitgift's brother, William, and concluded that the male line bearing the Whitgift name had long since died out. Not more than the occasional trace of the wider family remains in the historical record; George Whitgift's will, dated 1 May 1610, mentions a nephew and great-nephew of John Whitgift, both also bearing the name John.

In addition to commerce, another prominent influence within the family was religion. John Whitgift's uncle, Robert, had been elected Abbot of Wellow, in 1525, and he was to oversee the young boy's early education. Wellow was an Augustinian monastery, dating from the twelfth century, situated close to the coast south of Great Grimsby. Robert Whitgift had proved to be the last in the line of Abbots, as Wellow fell victim, in 1536, to the dissolution of the monasteries required by Henry VIII. It was subsequently destroyed, little more than its seal surviving. The medieval village, of which the monastery was the major part, covered a substantial acreage. It has, however, been entirely engulfed by modern Cleethorpes; the People's Park, located on part of the old Wellow Abbey estate, together with nearby Abbey Park Road, now feature on the site of Whitgift's earliest schooling. The buildings of the monastery, and its lands, passed to the Heneage family, wealthy local landowners, who acquired substantial quantities of former monastic land across Lincolnshire. Whitgift's career path was to overlap that of Sir Thomas Heneage, several decades later, when both men were members of the Privy Council from 1587, until Heneage's death in 1595. The Heneage family, unlike Whitgift's, continued to be influential, particularly in Lincolnshire, over the subsequent four centuries, with descendants representing local constituencies in Parliament, and one, Edward, the first Baron Heneage, holding the post of Chancellor of the Duchy of Lancaster in Gladstone's 1886 government.

The former Abbot was allowed to continue to reside at Wellow, after the monastery's dissolution, and the young Whitgift was invited by his uncle to join a number of other pupils being taught by him in what remained of the monastic buildings. It very soon became clear that the Whitgift family had the highest aspirations for the eldest son; his father was sufficiently impressed with the boy's potential to meet the expense of sending him to London, more than one hundred and seventy miles away, to attend St Anthony's School, located in the City between Broad Street and Threadneedle Street. St Anthony's had a reputation as one of London's finest schools, with probably around two hundred students, and many distinguished former pupils. These included John Colet, the Renaissance humanist and theologian, who became Dean of St Paul's Cathedral in 1505; Sir Thomas More, a fellow humanist and the ill-fated Lord Chancellor in Henry VIII's reign; and Nicholas Heath, Archbishop of York and also a Lord Chancellor, in the 1550s. John Colet's family background was very similar to Whitgift's, only wealthier, his merchant father being, twice, Lord Mayor of London. Whitgift's London education was made more affordable for his family by the fact that he was sent to lodge, at St Paul's Churchyard, with his aunt Isobel, wife of Michael Shaller, a verger at the Cathedral.

Whitgift would have followed a narrowly-defined educational programme, within a very strict disciplinary code, which entailed the acquisition of a prescribed body of knowledge, and the mastery of Latin and Greek, through the study of classical texts. Whitgift may well have sympathised with the somewhat lighter discipline later called for by Roger Ascham, tutor to Elizabeth I, as his library contained a copy of Ascham's *The Scholemaster*, published in 1570. In these formative years, Whitgift had the chance to follow an academic education of the highest quality. Crucially, he acquired a fluency in written and spoken Latin that was to provide the essential platform for his later career, during which he was regularly required to use it. The classical languages were very far from 'dead' in sixteenth-century England, and Whitgift's education in them would have spilled out of the schoolroom into local churches, and even onto the streets. On special occasions, including some Festival Days, masters from the various London schools organised formal debating competitions, with prizes for the top performers in disputing principles of grammar and points of logic. The boys continued these debates, in *impromptu* fashion, on the way to and from school. Disputes, of the kind later described by John Stow, in his book *A Survey of London*, commonly occurred between boys from St Anthony's and the more recently-founded St Paul's:

'the scholars of Paul's meeting with them of St Anthony's, would call them St Anthony's Pigs; and they again would call the other, Pigeons of Paul's; because many pigeons were bred in Paul's Church, and St Anthony was always figured with a pig following him: and mindful of the former usage, did for a long season (disorderly in the street) provoke one another with Salve: Salve tu quoque. Placet tibi mecum disputare? Placet. (Greetings: Greetings to you too. Will you agree to debate with me? I will) *And so proceeding from this to Questions in*

Grammar, they usually fell from words to blows, with their satchels full of books, many times in great heaps, that they troubled the streets and passengers'.

Making his way each day the half mile across London from St Paul's to St Anthony's, and back, Whitgift would have encountered scholars from other schools. But of his experiences, his application to study, or the 'derring-do' of his London schooldays, only the merest traces remain. Paule records an intriguing story: Whitgift, sharing a room with a fellow student, who had contracted the Plague, drank a pot of the boy's urine placed by the bed, thinking it was beer. The student died, but Whitgift emerged unscathed from the incident. There would have been more than a touch of the apocryphal here, though, for this story was taken to show, as John Strype, in his biography of Whitgift, commented, in the true spirit of Calvinist theories of predestination, *'divine Providence, by this preservation, had intended to reserve him for some great services in his Church afterwards'.*

Whitgift's schooling in London was cut short, probably during 1548. The commercial fortunes of his father's mercantile operations, out of Great Grimsby, appear to have dipped around this time, which could have imperilled Whitgift's ongoing education. However, it was to be a clash of personalities, and a divergence of religious beliefs, within his family, that led to a change of course. Whitgift's religious convictions did not match those of his aunt; he began to resist her requests to accompany her to the traditional Catholic Mass, and held to his refusal in the face of all efforts that were made to persuade him to comply. His furious aunt threw him out of her house, and sent him back to Great Grimsby. Her parting shot to Whitgift was, according to Paule, to whom Whitgift must have told the story, *'that she thought at the first, she had received a Saint into her house, but now she perceived he was a Devil'.* Her nephew was showing the force of character and determination to have his own way that were common themes as his career developed.

Whitgift returned to his family, for a very brief period, before a new chapter in his life began to unfold, with his departure for Cambridge. In sixteenth-century England, the road to high office in the Church, Whitgift's ultimate destination, passed through Oxford or Cambridge colleges. All six Archbishops of Canterbury, in the reigns of Henry VIII, Edward VI, Mary I, and Elizabeth I, were Oxbridge-educated. Five of them, William Warham, Thomas Cranmer, Matthew Parker, Edmund Grindal and John Whitgift himself, took the same route as the great Cardinal Wolsey before them, from modest merchant or farming backgrounds to the pinnacle of the national Church; only Reginald Pole, the last Roman Catholic Archbishop, was born into the nobility.

Commercial acumen, administrative and leadership ability, together with an openness to religion, were all in Whitgift's genes, or in his blood, as the sixteenth century would have phrased it. However, the skills he had developed, at Wellow Abbey and St

Anthony's, needed honing, and Cambridge now beckoned. Whitgift initially made his way to Queens' College, but found Pembroke Hall better suited to his aspirations, and formally moved to join that College, matriculating there in May 1550. The award of a Bible Clerkship recognised his ability and provided significant financial assistance, taking the pressure off his family's resources.

Pembroke was the perfect college for an ambitious, would-be cleric. Nicholas Ridley, Bishop of Rochester, and subsequently of London, was its distinguished Master. He was a reformist figure, at the cutting edge of the English Reformation, a leading advocate of the establishment of a national Church. He was also a close ally of Thomas Cranmer, whom he assisted in the compilation of the seminal *Book of Common Prayer*. Edmund Grindal, the future Archbishop of Canterbury, was a highly-influential Fellow of Pembroke. Whitgift's personal tutor at the College was John Bradford, 'Holy Bradford', seen by many in Cambridge as a saintly figure, a man totally committed to Edwardian Protestantism. An unwavering belief in the worth and rectitude of an established, national Church became a defining characteristic of Whitgift's religious beliefs. The intense, intellectual atmosphere of Cambridge, in the mid sixteenth century, must have been far more intoxicating, for the young man from Great Grimsby, than the small beer of his London schooldays.

Whitgift was just entering his twenties when his family circumstances were altered by the death of his father, Henry. The will, proved in October 1552, shows a family still living in comfort; as the eldest son, Whitgift might have expected to inherit substantially more than his siblings, but that seems not to have been the case, property being divided amongst the six sons, and left in trust for the younger brothers. His mother was bequeathed no property, just £15 in cash, and the use of the family house and furniture while she remained unmarried. Henry Whitgift's donations to charity and the local church totalled 52 pence, a very modest sum, contrasting sharply with the huge endowment of land and property that Whitgift himself wrote into his own will, in 1596, for his Foundation in Croydon. Whitgift did receive one personal gift from his father, described in the will as *'my best gowne and my best dublytt of taffataye* (silk doublet)'.

The accession to the English throne, in 1553, of a Catholic, Mary Tudor, determined to re-establish the authority of the Pope, and the former links with Rome, ushered in a highly-dangerous, six-year period for Whitgift, for whom such a policy was anathema. The two Cambridge men, Bradford and Ridley, who at this point had had the greatest influence on the young Whitgift, were now imprisoned, in the Tower of London; both were subsequently burnt at the stake, as heretics, the former in July, the latter in October, 1555. A man of Whitgift's intelligence and reformist views, who already, in his teens, had stubbornly refused to accompany his aunt to a 'Popish' Mass, might have met the same fate. He was no longer a mere student, having progressed his studies to the degree of Bachelor of Arts, and been elected a Fellow of Peterhouse, Cambridge, in May of that year. Cardinal Pole, as Papal Legate and Chancellor of the University, was about to lead a Visitation of Cambridge, seeking to root out opponents of Marian religious doctrines, and Whitgift would have been very much of interest to the inspecting authorities.

That Whitgift was not martyred for his Protestant beliefs, in the mid-1550s, perhaps owed as much to good fortune as to his own judgment. A life-threatening illness, which struck soon after his change of college, ironically helped to save him. He was cared for, in a house near the College; all necessary arrangements for his recovery were overseen by the Master of Peterhouse, Dr Andrew Perne, who guaranteed to underwrite the expenses of Whitgift's care. Once Whitgift recovered, Dr Perne provided another significant form of potentially life-saving assistance. Restored to health, Paule records that Whitgift

'determined to travel beyond the seas, purposely to avoid certain Visitors sent in Queen Mary's time to the University, to establish Popery…Dr Perne hearing of this his purpose, talked with him, and found him resolute in his religion…whereupon the Doctor willed him to be silent, and not troublesome in uttering his opinion, whereby others might take occasion to call him in question: and he for his part, would wink at him, and so order the matter, that he might continue his religion and not travel out of the University'.

This was a key moment in the young Whitgift's career. Dr Perne had undertaken to 'turn a blind eye' to Whitgift's beliefs, and to provide the essential cover to obscure him from view. Cardinal Pole arrived in Cambridge, in 1556, seeking to suppress heresy and enforce compliance with Catholic doctrine. Whitgift was shielded, by Perne, from any close enquiries of the kind that led to John Hullier, a Norfolk clergyman, being burnt at the stake on Jesus Green, Cambridge, in April, having refused to renounce his Protestant faith. Even the dead were not to be left undisturbed; the bodies of the German Protestant theologians, Paul Fagius and Martin Bucer, buried in Cambridge, were dug up and burnt, together with their books. Perne was the perfect ally for Whitgift in these precarious times, an archetypal 'Vicar of Bray' figure, happy to advocate Catholic doctrines, recant, embrace them again, and then finally renounce them, as he did through the reigns of Henry VIII, Edward VI, Mary I and Elizabeth I, respectively. Extraordinarily, it was to be Perne who was Vice-Chancellor of the University, in 1560, when Fagius and Bucer were re-buried with honour in Cambridge, Perne having held the same office, four years earlier, when they were exhumed. With Perne's assistance, Whitgift was able to remain safely in Cambridge throughout Mary's reign. While some later sought to impugne Perne's motives for providing this help, and Puritans derided Whitgift as *'Perne's boy'*, labelling Perne himself *'Old Turner'*, and *'Judas Perne'*, Whitgift himself showed a deep, personal gratitude. The two men remained close friends through the rest of their lives, when Perne was Dean of Ely as well as Master of Peterhouse for more than three decades.

Perne also remained influential in Whitgift's rise in the Church. He stayed at Lambeth Palace in his old age, during Whitgift's term as Archbishop of Canterbury, and died there in 1589.

Any threat to Whitgift's life was finally dispelled, in November 1558, with the accession of Elizabeth I. He felt at ease with the concept of a national religion that the Queen was insisting should be adopted. Whitgift took Holy Orders in 1560, and preached his first sermon shortly afterwards, at Great St Mary's, in Cambridge, taking as his text Romans, Chapter 1, *'I am not ashamed of the Gospel of Christ'*. His reputation and his income were advancing in equal measure. He now came under the patronage of another influential figure, Dr Richard Cox, the Bishop of Ely, one of the Marian exiles, who, unlike Whitgift, had escaped abroad to Antwerp and Frankfurt to avoid persecution. As well as benefitting from the ongoing support of Perne, in Cambridge and Ely, Whitgift could, through association with Bishop Cox, add significantly to his range of important contacts. Cox had been Chancellor of the University of Oxford, as well as in close touch with many other Marian exiles. He made Whitgift one of his personal Chaplains. He also recommended him for the living of the Rectory at Teversham, just a few miles from Cambridge, which gave Whitgift another significant financial boost. Cox was both hostile to Roman Catholicism and a determined enemy of the Puritans, and remained as Bishop in Ely for more than two decades. In addition to being a useful ally, he served as an exemplar for various policies that Whitgift chose to adopt, as Bishop and Archbishop, including a single-minded determination to maximise the income available to him, to underpin a successful career and to support his charitable purposes.

(Opposite) The Wellow Abbey seal, attached to a parchment document, dated 10 September 1471, in Grimsby Archives.

(Left) The view along the River Ouse, from the Church of St Mary Magdalene, in Whitgift

(Below, left) The Church of St Mary Magdalene, in Whitgift village

(Below, right) The commemorative plaque marking John Whitgift's birthplace, at 37/39 Bethlehem Street, Grimsby

(Opposite) Grimsby Minster

Grimsby, Cleethorpes & District Civic Society

Born here
on Bethlehem Street, this
son of a local merchant was
educated at nearby Wellow Abbey
JOHN WHITGIFT
1530-1604
Became Archbishop of Canterbury
and the most trusted confidante
of Queen Elizabeth I

Grimsby Heritage Walking Trail

(Top) The modern port of Grimsby

(Left) The People's Park, Grimsby, on the site of Wellow Abbey's estate

(Opposite)
A schoolmaster, brandishing his birch cane, with pupils, in an early sixteenth-century manuscript

2

Master of Trinity

In the early 1560s, Whitgift was emerging as one of the leading academics of his generation in Cambridge. In 1563, he became Lady Margaret Professor of Divinity. He chose *'The Pope is the Anti-Christ'* as the text for his first Address, reflecting a more forthright and confident style. His impact, through the quality of his lectures and preaching, led to the stipend for his professorship being increased by 50%, from twenty marks to £20 per annum, in July 1566.

In January 1567, Bishop Horne of Winchester recommended Whitgift to Sir William Cecil, Secretary of State and the Queen's chief adviser, for appointment as Dean of Canterbury. Horne described Whitgift as *'a man honest and very well learned'*. Whitgift was not selected for the post; it went instead to Thomas Godwin, an Oxford-educated cleric whose talent as a preacher had already come under royal scrutiny. Had Whitgift been selected, he would all but certainly have had a lesser career than the one that awaited him. Dean of Canterbury was not then, and has subsequently proved only occasionally, a route to the most senior post in the Church. It had been to Whitgift's advantage that he was just behind Godwin in the 'pecking order' at the time, as he was about to climb to the highest branches of the Cambridge academic tree. In the course of 1567, Whitgift first became Master of his old college, Pembroke, then, within a few months, moved, to become the Master of a major, recently-founded college, Trinity, and to take up the post of Regius Professor of Divinity.

He wrote to thank Cecil, Chancellor of Cambridge University, for his support in these Cambridge appointments, and for showing faith in him in the face of criticism, in some quarters, of his appointment to Trinity. The move to a wealthier college, and his enhanced remuneration, would come just in time, Whitgift claimed, in a letter to Cecil:

'That preferment that I have, whatsoever it is, I have it by your Honour his means. And therefore I owe myself wholly unto you. But it is not so much as it is reported. The mastership of Pembroke Hall is but £4 the year and 18d in the week for commons. My benefice [Teversham Rectory] *is one of the least in al the dioces. My Lecture* [the Lady Margaret Professorship] *is the whole stay of my lyving. My debts are more than I shal ever, being in the state I am, be able to discharge. And extreme necessity, not any prodigalitie, hath brought me into them…'*

Whitgift was often at pains to try to convince others that his income was not as high as they might think. Why he was now finding it so difficult to live off a sum that should have sufficed very comfortably for a single man, with accommodation provided, is uncertain. As Percy points out, it is likely that, as a consequence of his father's death, he was financially responsible for the education of his younger brothers, two of whom were admitted to study at Peterhouse in Cambridge, in 1560 and 1561; the youngest brother, Geoffrey, was later admitted to Trinity, as a scholar, when Whitgift was Master. However, Whitgift had sufficient surplus resources, in 1565, to purchase Curles, a house at Clavering in Essex, twenty miles from Cambridge, to provide a retreat for himself and a home for his brother, William; he may well have inherited from his uncle, Robert, who had died in January that year.

Whitgift's smooth, swift rise came about, as he had been quick to acknowledge, thanks to the patronage of Cecil, but also, in no small part, because Whitgift too, like other promising young men before him, had, with Cecil's support, come to the attention of the Queen. Paule notes:

'His singular, and extraordinary gift in preaching, caused him…to be sent for to preach before Her Majesty, who took so great liking of him, for his method, and matter, that, hearing his name to be Whitgift, she said he had a white-gift indeed. And as his gifts were then esteemed white, so his fortune afterwards proved white, and happy; his good name and reputation white, and spotless: so that it may be properly said of him, that he was gallinae filius albae ("the son of a white hen", regarded as highly auspicious, certain to bring good fortune).

This was indeed a strong indication of royal approval. Elizabeth was a gifted scholar herself, and, like Whitgift, fluent in Latin and Greek, so she had a background of her own against which to measure his talent, and great confidence in her ability to do so. She enjoyed teasing those around her, showing her skill in punning word-play; the play the Queen made on Whitgift's *'white gifts'* confirmed the positive impression he had made. At the Queen's invitation, he became one of her Chaplains; what was to be a key relationship influencing the later decades of his life had begun in perfect fashion.

Trinity College, to which Whitgift moved, as Master, on 4 July 1567, had been founded by Henry VIII, in 1546, the principal aim being to safeguard the religious reforms of Henry's reign by developing leaders for the English Church. Trinity had taken over the buildings of the old King's Hall and Michaelhouse institutions, dating from the early fourteenth century. The new College had a very wealthy endowment, the majority drawn from dissolved religious houses, and estates purchased by the King. Whitgift left architectural development to his successors, but set about other aspects of institutional reform. There was great authoritarian potential in the hands of a strong Head of House, and Whitgift exploited it to the full. He expected the highest standards of application to their studies from the Trinity College students; Paule records:

'he usually dined and supped in the Common-Hall, as well to have a watchful eye over the scholars, and to keep them in a mannerly and awful obedience, as by his example, to teach them to be contented with a scholar-like College diet.'

We are told that Whitgift insisted that the Trinity scholars adhered

'to their public disputations, and exercises, and prayers, which he never missed, chiefly for devotion, and withal to observe others absence, always severly punishing such omissions and negligences.'

In showing himself to be a stern disciplinarian, Whitgift was revealing an important aspect of his character that the Queen would value highly later in her reign, at the height of what she saw as the Puritan threat to her Church. As Whitgift himself expressed it, to the Cambridge Chancellor, Cecil:

'I may not suffer those with whom I do to disquiet the university or college with false doctrine and schismatical opinions: I may not suffer them openly to break and contemn those laws and statutes which they are sworn to observe, and I to execute...these be the

things I have done, and these be the things that I intend to do; whereby as hitherto I have kept the place where I am in some quiet and good order, so do I trust to continue it.'

The Puritan, Giles Wigginton, a scholar and Fellow of the College, was one who complained that he had been the victim of *'hard dealinge'*, and that the Master was always unfairly seeking out *'such scholars and boys as durst be bold to reprove sin and call for reformation…*[calling them] *saucy boys, busy bodies and meddlers'*. Wigginton remained on Whitgift's 'radar,' and in the 1580s, when a clergyman in Sedbergh, he was pursued by Whitgift and the church commissioners for breaches of regulations, Whitgift involving himself personally in the prosecutions; Wigginton was deprived of his living, and served spells of imprisonment.

Whitgift had his opponents, and there were many who advocated Puritan beliefs in Cambridge, but he was also widely respected, and many Fellows and students of Trinity became his life-long friends. The reputation of the College itself was transformed. G M Trevelyan, a former student, emphasises that it was during Whitgift's time as Master that Trinity, previously seen as an offshoot of St John's, *'became its rival on equal terms … *[and] *also began to educate a large proportion of the leaders of the new era'*. Edward Coke, who was to become the most distinguished lawyer of his generation, was admitted to Trinity in 1567; Francis Bacon, the complete 'Renaissance man', and one of the leading figures of the age, became an undergraduate in 1573; and, in 1577, the Earl of Essex, later the brilliant, but ill-starred, favourite of Queen Elizabeth, was taken into the Master's Lodgings as his own pupil, albeit briefly, by Whitgift. Essex was to develop what one contemporary, Sir Henry Wotton, Secretary to the Earl from 1595 to 1600, called *'a kind of filial reverence towards Dr Whitgift'*. A close link was established between the two men, despite differences on religion, where Essex developed strong Puritan sympathies. It was a friendship that would last throughout Essex's life, with only an occasional blip, until his tragic demise, in which Whitgift was to play an important part. Other sons of aristocratic families, such as the Earls of Worcester and Cumberland, Lord Zouch, and Lord Dunboy of Ireland, were all drawn to study at Trinity because of the excellent reputation the College was achieving under Whitgift's leadership.

Further evidence of Whitgift's exceptional attention to detail is provided by an account book, now in Lambeth Palace Library, with entries in his own handwriting, recording expenditure on dozens of his pupils. For George Clifford, the third Earl of Cumberland, aged just thirteen, Whitgift lists his personal outgoings, for recovery later from the boy's guardian: the costs of paper, an hour glass, a zither lute, a comb, a series of breakfasts, shoeing the boy's horse, caring for and cleaning his clothes, and purchasing books.

There were, however, far more significant matters to be addressed in Cambridge than shoeing horses or purchasing paper. Theological debate in the University, in the sixteenth century, both reflected and shaped some of the most important contemporary issues of Church and State. However, disputes which then were vigorously and passionately pursued seem now as dry as dust; blinkered, bigoted views, expounded in highly-politicised debates, reflecting bitter, intense, personal rivalries. Matters seen by contemporaries as of the utmost importance to life, liberty and conscience appear now, from a twenty-first century perspective, to be peripheral, irrelevant or self-indulgent, trapped in a very particular time-warp. Sadly, this would be amply confirmed by any close reading of the three volumes of *The Works of Archbishop John Whitgift*, published in 1851; immense, painstaking labours and considerable skill expended, over hundreds of thousands of words, by Whitgift, one of the ablest clerics of his day, developing arguments that had little, if any, lasting impact.

Whitgift largely kept apart from the often-lethal debating frenzies in religion in the 1550s and 1560s. He did not take Holy Orders until after Elizabeth's accession, which had seemed to ensure the defeat of Catholicism. With one exception, he did not become embroiled in the vestiarian controversy, the seemingly-endless disputes about which vestments should be worn by clergymen officiating in services, which clerical dress best reflected Christianity's origins, and its core beliefs. To wear or not to wear a surplice, a square cap, or a round cap, just as when to kneel, or when to make the sign of the cross, were fiercely-contested issues, plaguing much of the sixteenth century, costing many clergymen their livings, and some their lives.

Whitgift had shown a sure touch through a divisive and dangerous period. There had been just the one, wrong-footed moment. In November 1565, Whitgift joined Matthew Hutton, the Cambridge Regius Professor of Divinity, and some of the Heads of College in Cambridge, in calling for moderation, and some freedom of choice, in the vestiarian dispute. Hutton was a friend and an exact contemporary of Whitgift, a graduate and Fellow of Trinity, and the two men would have known each other's views very well. But they were to make a major mistake. They signed up to a letter, sent by the Heads to Cecil, calling for greater tolerance of varieties of practice in the wearing of vestments. As Strype summarises the response of Cecil and key Privy Counsellors, the letter was '*very ill-taken...as moving a matter very unseasonable and injurious to the state of learning there* [in Cambridge]'. Whitgift decided to beat a hasty retreat from an untenable position. However, even two years later, on the eve of taking up his Trinity College Mastership, he was still having to assure Secretary of State Cecil of his loyalty, and his commitment to conformity. Whitgift was exasperated by what he felt were unfair, repeated assertions, in certain quarters, to the contrary:

'…It is not unknown unto me, what is reported of me unto your Honour…For God's sake, let it be judged what I am by my doings, and not by the report of those, who do not to me as they would themselves be done unto. As touching my not-conformity (which is one thing layd against me), I dare be judged by my Lord of Canterbury his Grace, your Honour, or my Lord of London, or Master Dean of York: who knoweth more of my mind in this matter than any man doth beside. I never encouraged any to withstand the Queen's Majesties laws in that behalf; but I both have, and do by al I may, seek to persuade men to conform themselves.'

Whitgift had learnt a sharp lesson; not for thirty years would he make another significant mistake, with the unsuccessful attempt to enforce his Lambeth Articles of 1595.

His commitment to conformity in religion emphasised, Whitgift was now about to be thrust onto centre stage in a major tussle with the Puritans, which was to become a *cause célèbre* of the 1570s. Whitgift's successor, as Lady Margaret Professor of Divinity, had been an ally, William Chaderton, who, in turn, had succeeded him as Regius Professor in Cambridge. But, in Chaderton's place as Lady Margaret Professor, in 1569, came Thomas Cartwright, who was rapidly to emerge as Whitgift's arch-enemy. One of the most talented Puritans of the age, Cartwright was a close contemporary of Whitgift; the historian, Dawley, points out that they graduated together, in 1554, Whitgift twentieth and Cartwright thirty-fourth on a Cambridge University degree list. Cartwright had become a Fellow of Trinity, and his views on church government were certain to put him swiftly at odds with the Master, and with the ecclesiastical establishment in general.

Cartwright was a gifted preacher, and a strong critic of the structure of the Elizabethan Church. But, in Whitgift, he more than met his match; Whitgift was irritated and angered by what had become constant, internecine warfare in religion, and he was convinced of the threat to the national Church that inaction would pose. Whitgift led his fellow Heads of College in a reform of university governance, designed to give them more power to tackle opposition and to prevent a drift towards anarchic discord. He was the driving force behind new statutes for the University in 1570, and an Act of Parliament in 1571. The statutes by which the University was governed were revised, to give College Heads greater authority, including the power to choose the Vice-Chancellor, and control nominations to the annually-elected representative body, the Caput. Undergraduates were now required to be members of a college, and three years residence was made obligatory, as was the study of classics, arithmetic, rhetoric and logic. The reforms overseen by Whitgift were long-lasting, but Cartwright was their immediate target. The revised statutes gave the Vice-Chancellor the power to summon and investigate any preacher whose sermons were, in his view, subversive, or who was deemed to be in opposition to the religious establishment. Any preacher could be required, by the Vice-Chancellor, to revoke his preaching and conform, or, on refusing, could be expelled from the University.

Cartwright had used the Lady Margaret Professorship to give himself a new platform from which to preach the advantages of the more primitive organisation of the early Christian Church, and the authority of congregations, when compared to the Episcopalian system of archbishops and bishops in Elizabethan England. With the administrative changes in place, Whitgift was the natural choice of his fellow Heads of College for the key role of Vice-Chancellor, to see the reforms established; he was to serve two terms, 1570-1 and 1573-4. One of his first acts was to deprive Cartwright of his Professorship, and to remove him from his Trinity Fellowship. Another prominent Puritan, Walter Travers, left Trinity to avoid a similar expulsion; Whitgift wrote:

'I was forced, by due punishment so to weary him, till he was fain to travel and depart from the college to Geneva, otherwise he should have been expelled for want of conformity towards the orders of the house, and for his pertinancy'.

Cartwright too chose to have a brief spell in Geneva, licking his wounds after his ejection from Trinity; he returned, in 1572, spoiling for a fight. In June that year, two leading Puritans, John Field and Thomas Wilcox, published an anonymous tract, entitled *An Admonition to the Parliament*. It called for wholesale restructuring in religion, to follow a pattern set by the scriptures, to rid the Church of what were described as all its Papist aspects, and return it to its origins:

'remove Advowsons, Patronages, Impropriations, and bishoppes' authoritie…Take away the Lordship, the loitering, the pompe, the idleness, and livings of Bishops, but yet employ them to such ends as they were in the old churche appointed for…look that they preache, not quarterly or monthly, but continually: not for filthy lucre's sake but of a ready mynde'.

Cartwright warmly supported the *Admonition*, which therefore pitched him immediately into a new and bitter dispute with Whitgift. A seemingly interminable war of words ensued between Cartwright and the Master of Trinity, and their respective allies, sermon and counter-sermon, accusation, refutation and counter-accusation. Whitgift published a detailed response to the *Admonition*, entitled *An Answer to a Certain Libel*, taking great pains to refute his opponent's assertions, point by point; Cartwright then penned a *Reply to an Answer made of Doctor Whitgift against the Admonition to the Parliament*; Whitgift published *A Defence of the Answer*; Cartwright responded with his *Second Reply*. Whitgift wrote to Burghley to assure him that

'convenient discipline, joined with doctrine, being duly executed, will soon remedy all… sects and schisms cannot, by any means, endure these two.'

Whitgift was as infuriated by what he saw as Cartwright's contemptuous style of writing, as by its content:

'…any man of judgment that readeth his book may easily perceive, with what haughtiness of mind, what contempt and disdain of others, in what slanderous and opprobrious manner it is written. How oft doth he repeat "M.Doctor," in contempt either of the degree or of the person! 370 times is the least. What other speeches of disdain and reproach doth he utter!'

The essence of Cartwright's position was that only a presbyterian order, church government by assemblies, not by individuals, was rooted in scripture, and therefore this was the only legitimate form. Whitgift's standpoint was diametrically opposed; in his view, the argument that

'matters of ceremonies, discipline, and kind of government [are] *necessary to salvation is a doctrine strange and unheard of to me… This church of England abandoned great numbers of papistical rites and ceremonies; but, because it refuseth some, may it therefore retain none? Or, because it rejecteth those which be wicked and unprofitable, may it not therefore keep still such as be godly and pertain to order and decency?'*

In Whitgift's opinion, there would always be those who would find fault:

'I know that no church can be so perfect in all points of external government and ceremonies, but that such as be disposed may pick some occasion of quarrelling thereat, though unjustly.'

This particular battle had been fought to a standstill, and Cartwright had alienated too many people to have any chance of re-establishing himself in Cambridge. He went abroad again, seeking more sympathetic environments. Whitgift, who had found Cartwright's impact at Trinity *'marvellous troublesome and contentious'*, would have been delighted to see him depart. When Cartwright returned, his colourful career continued, in the 1580s and 1590s, with the imposition of terms of imprisonment before, surprisingly, he settled down to conclude his life quietly, in some comfort, as Master of the Earl of Leicester's Hospital, in Warwick. What would have been even harder to predict, however, was that Cartwright and Whitgift would make peace, and be at ease in each other's company. Paule records the mutual respect that he observed developing in the 1590s, and credits Whitgift with securing Cartwright's release from a term of imprisonment in the Fleet jail, in 1591:

'For which, and sundry other his favours, Master Cartwright held himself much obliged unto him, as he confessed in his letters…In which letters he is also pleased to vouchsafe him [Whitgift] *the stile of a Right Reverend Father in God, and his Lord the Archbishop's Grace of Canterbury. Which title of Grace he also often yieldeth him throughout his letters…Yea the Archbishop hath been heard to say, that if Master Cartwright had not so far ingaged himself as he did in the beginning, he thought verily he would in his latter time have been drawn to conformity. For when he was freed from his troubles, he often repaired to the Archbishop, who used him kindly, and was contented to tolerate his preaching in Warwick divers years, upon his promise, that he would not impugn the laws, orders, and government in this Church of England'.*

(Opposite) Whitgift's coat of arms, on Queen's Gate, Trinity College, Cambridge

29

(Above) A portrait of
Doctor Whitgift, in
his late thirties, from
Peterhouse, Cambridge

(Left) Hammond's
plan of Cambridge,
dated 1592

(Opposite) Great St
Mary's, The University
Church, Cambridge

Mr. THO: CARTWRIGHT.

(Opposite) Portrait of   *(Above) Whitgift's*
John Whitgift, when   *Puritan adversary,*
Master of Trinity   *Thomas Cartwright*
College, Cambridge

3

The Road to Canterbury

'*Cometh the hour, cometh the man*'; the final stages of Whitgift's ascent to the pinnacle of the Elizabethan Church have an inexorable feel. Whitgift was intellectually strong, less pedantic and more pragmatic than many contemporaries, a committed disciplinarian, a confident leader happy to speak his mind and scornful of popularity; he possessed the perfect credentials for what the Queen was seeking to achieve, good order in the Church, and unity in place of discord. He had remained under royal observation, the most significant opportunity to remind the Queen of his '*white gifts*' coming in March 1574, when he preached a sermon in her presence at Greenwich; it was subsequently printed with the title '*A Godly Sermon*'. Whitgift's text this time was from John, Chapter 6, '*Labour not for the meat which perisheth, but for the meat which endureth unto everlasting life*'. Biblical quotation, allusion and interpretation flow one after another through a lengthy text. Whitgift mixed intelligence in argument, and detail in illustration, showing himself at ease with the Latin and Greek texts, in a classical style which would have appealed to the Queen's intellect.

Whitgift's career took another sharp, upward turn in 1577, out of Cambridge. Having previously been discussed, in 1575, as a possible candidate to become Bishop of Norwich, he was chosen to succeed Nicholas Bullingham as Bishop of Worcester. Whitgift was to prove the fifth incumbent to hold the Bishopric *en route* to Canterbury, the first being Dunstan, 957-9, the most recent Thomas Bourchier, in the mid fifteenth century.

The University Church, Great St Mary's, in Cambridge, was packed for Whitgift's final sermon, in which, in contrast to earlier orations, he urged reconciliation. At a private sermon, in Trinity College, on giving up the Mastership, Paule records that

'he gave unto that Society such a godly and learned exhortation for their continuance and constancy in peace and unity, as it so moved their affections, that they burst out into tears, insomuch that there were scarce any dry eyes to be found amongst the whole number. He chose for his text the same farewell which St Paul gave to the Corinthians; Finally brethren, fare you well: Be perfect, be of good comfort, be of one mind, live in peace...'

Many of the Heads of College and leading figures of the University joined a huge cavalcade, in June 1577, to escort Whitgift out of Cambridge on the first leg of his journey, of more than one hundred miles, westwards to Worcester; interestingly, despite the exceptional impact the University had had on his career, and although he continued to show an interest in the University's affairs, he never returned. The influence he continued to have in Cambridge was exercised principally through friends and protégés, such as one of his former Chaplains, John Copcot, who became Vice-Chancellor in 1586.

Whitgift was travelling along a golden road, and in the process of becoming one of the wealthier pluralists of his time. His accumulation of office, both ecclesiastical and secular, drew Puritan scorn, but his personal wealth and influence were growing apace. While Master at Trinity, he had continued to benefit from his close association with Richard Cox, Bishop of Ely, becoming, in 1568, a Prebend and Canon of Ely. Whitgift went on to swap his Teversham living for another, wealthier living in Laceby, Lincolnshire, and his Ely post to be a Prebend of Nassington, attached to Lincoln Cathedral. He also held the post of Dean of Lincoln, from 1571 to 1577. In 1571, he was chosen to preach at Convocation, the ecclesiastical assembly, and was, as Dean, elected Prolocutor of the Lower House, in 1572. He spent some time each year at the Old Deanery in Lincoln, which enjoyed an attractive location above the city.

Whitgift was determined to maximize the income available to him, as Bishop of Worcester, in the same way that his mentor, Cox, had done in Ely. He was always on his guard against the inevitability of laymen seeking to despoil the Church, as he had written to Cox in December 1575:

'[The laity] *does envy any prosperity in the clergy, what enemies the most part of men are to cathedral churches, bishopricks, colleges, and other places of learning...the temporality seek to make the clergy beggars, that we may depend upon them'.*

He was able to make the perfect start in Worcester, in increasing his resources, due to two exceptional examples of royal favour: first, the Queen allowed her new Bishop to retain for himself the *'first fruits and tenths'* of his office, waving her right to receive a significant portion of his income during his first year in office; second, she allowed him to control patronage in the Worcester Diocese, which had previously been reserved to the Crown, to appoint the Prebends in his Cathedral and to nominate the Justices of the Peace for Worcestershire and Warwickshire.

Whitgift turned immediately to administrative and financial reform. He was frustrated at what he saw as the errors of his predecessors in granting long leases on manors, parks and mansions in the ownership of the See; this was inevitably more striking to a new incumbent, particularly at a time of significant price inflation. An example of Whitgift's determination to try to gain every penny that he felt he was due can be seen in his protracted tussle with a man named Abington, over income from two manors, Hollowe and Grimley. As Whitgift saw it, this income was *'the chief upholding of the Bishop's hospitality, and without which (especially in dear years) he is not able to keep house'*. When Abington resisted the pressure he was exerting, Whitgift turned to powerful figures at Court, the Earl of Leicester, Sir Christopher Hatton and Sir Francis Walsingham, to help him get his way. Whitgift sought the support of Cecil, created Lord Burghley in February 1571, to enable a successful outcome to his tenacious struggle to cling on to Hartlebury Castle, the Bishop of Worcester's official residence, when the powers of a royal commission were being used to question his rights of ownership. Whitgift was also active in strictly limiting the level of arrears that his tenants could build up, and in enforcing evictions where they would not, or could not, pay.

Whitgift took advantage of the timber available in woods belonging to the Bishopric, a resource Bishops were often accused of exploiting. He utilised part of his income to carry out extensive repairs to Church property. He was also keen to emphasise ecclesiastical authority and dignity alike, by having an impressive household, maintaining a large retinue of servants, and travelling around the Diocese, on certain occasions, with great ceremony. Bells would be rung in the towns to announce the arrival of the Bishop's extensive train of followers, as he progressed through the County. Whitgift's wealth enabled him to exercise subtler forms of influence, through hospitality and the entertainment of Judges, Justices of the Peace and local gentry at the Assize and Quarter Session courts in Worcester, and on other important occasions. Paule stressed not just the wealth that Whitgift accumulated, but the good that he did, in a variety of ways, for his Diocese:

'when he was Bishop of Worcester, unless extraordinary businesses of the Marches of Wales hindred him, he never failed to preach upon every Sabbath-day; many times riding five or six

miles to a parish church, and after sermon, came home to dinner…he did exceeding good by that his continual preaching, as also by his often conference, and conventing of the Papists'.

Many contemporaries, from the Queen down, recognised Whitgift's gifts as a preacher, but, while much may have come naturally to him, Paule stressed Whitgift's methodical approach:

'He never preached, but he first wrote his notes in Latin, and afterwards kept them during his life. For he would say, that whosoever took that pains before his preaching, the elder he waxed, the better he should discharge that duty; but if he trusted only to his memory, his preaching in time would become pratling.'

Paule also drew attention to Whitgift's skills of reconciliation in Worcester. When feuding between two members of the local gentry, Sir John Russell and Sir Henry Berkeley, came to a head, both arrived in Worcester with their armed supporters, and

'great bloodshed was likely to have ensued…had not the Bishop wisely prevented it, by providing a strong watch at the gates, and about the City, and requiring them to bring both parties, with their attendance, well guarded to his Palace, where he caused them all to the number of four or five hundred, to deliver their weapons into his own servants custody; and after two hours pains taken, sometimes in persuading, and otherwhiles in threatning them, he made them so good friends, as they both attended him hand in hand to the Town Hall… in amity and love, and ever after held him in great honour and estimation'.

Whitgift faced issues with both Catholics and Puritans, but, in this Bishopric, the former were perceived as being a greater problem than the latter. Catholic priests, arriving in England from the Continent, after training at seminary colleges such as Douai or Rheims, were regarded as posing a threat to the Church. Whitgift had a recent royal proclamation of July 1580, against traitors, and the 1581 parliamentary statute, designed *'to retain the Queen's Majesty's subjects in their due obedience'*, to take into account. Recusants, those who refused to attend the services of the national Chuch, even with the minimum frequency required to conform, particularly Catholics, were a target. Failing to attend the parish church brought liability to a fine of £20 per month, and hearing mass could be punished with a fine of one hundred marks (about £66). Members of noble and gentry families across the country were often ignored, although Whitgift was sent a list of names by the Privy Council of those who were to be investigated.

Whitgift's administrative talent led to him being called upon to draw up new statutes for Hereford Cathedral, and to a commission being issued for him to visit the Diocese of Lichfield and Coventry to sort out financial and other difficulties. He also had the opportunity to demonstrate his worth, as a servant of the Crown, on his appointment as Vice President of the Council of Wales and the Marches. The Council, which was based chiefly in Ludlow, had responsibilities across Wales and in the English counties of Shropshire, Gloucestershire, Herefordshire and Worcestershire. The President of the Council, Sir Henry Stanley, was at this time absent with his duties as Lord Deputy of Ireland. Whitgift was therefore drawn into overseeing the full range of Council business, including murders, felonies and disturbances of the peace, piracy and wrecking, enclosure and manorial disputes, common law appeals, corruption and false verdicts of juries. In addition to all of these civil burdens, Whitgift also had responsibility for administering the laws on religion.

Unsurprisingly, he proved up to the task, and well capable of the attention to detail and huge commitment of time required. He was especially active against corrupt officials, and any laxity in enforcing the laws against Catholic recusants. Frequent reports were made to the Privy Council in London, which in turn gave Whitgift additional powers, including the authority to use torture on recusants if he saw fit. The Lord President, Stanley, was less impressed, and jealous of his personal authority; relations between the two men became strained. Stanley complained to the Privy Council about shortcomings during his absence, and at not being kept fully informed by Whitgift as to the conduct of his Vice Presidential activities, claims that Whitgift strongly rebutted.

Towards the end of his time in Worcester, Whitgift had the benefit of the support of a new ally, Richard Cosin, who had been one of his scholars at Trinity College, Cambridge. Cosin was a gifted ecclesiastical lawyer, and was to be an important figure during Whitgift's time as Archbishop of Canterbury. He appointed him Chancellor of the Diocese of Worcester in 1582. It was on Cosin's watch, as Chancellor of Whitgift's ecclesiastical consistory court in Worcester, that the bond for William Shakespeare's marriage to Anne Hathaway (seemingly erroneously listed by a clerk as 'Whateley'), was recorded, in the Episcopal Register, in November 1582.

On the death of Edmund Grindal, in 1583, Whitgift was the personal choice of the Queen to succeed him as Archbishop of Canterbury. She knew Whitgift's strengths and talent, he would be her man, on whom she could depend, to ensure the security of her Church in dangerous times. He also had one additional quality, in the Queen's eyes, which his two closest potential rivals for the Archbishopric, Edwin Sandys, Archbishop of York, and John Aylmer, Bishop of London, could not match: they were married men, Whitgift was unmarried, like the Queen herself, and she strongly disapproved, in principle, of married clergy.

Whitgift would therefore begin his leadership of the Church with two huge advantages: he had the support and confidence of the Queen, as a trump card to use against any opponents, and to counter-balance the influence of Elizabeth's chief counsellor, Burghley;

and his two predecessors as Archbishop had both fallen a long way short of the Queen's high expectations. In Matthew Parker, Elizabeth didn't get exactly what she wanted; in his successor, Edmund Grindal, she got exactly what she didn't want. Parker had seemed a strong choice, but had been, initially, unwilling to undertake the role. He had been widely seen, on appointment, as a moderate figure, so it was perhaps inevitable, given his particular generation, that he would prove a disappointment. To Whitgift's great advantage, Edmund Grindal, Parker's successor, although only at Canterbury for less than eight years, had been an almost total disaster. He had failed woefully to achieve the conformity in religious practice that Elizabeth desired. He had also been unable even to secure certain specific policy objectives, such as preventing 'prophesyings', the discussion meetings held by Puritan clergy that were feared to be hotbeds of opposition to the established Church, and to authority in general. Grindal's weakness had led the Queen initially to try to persuade him to resign his post, and then to sequestrate his appointment, and to suspend him from all jurisdiction, for a six-year period, from 1577.

There had, therefore, been a power vacuum at the head of the Church in England, a perfect background for the strong-willed and confident cleric who would now take up the reins. Whitgift knew it would be no easy task, however, and looked for divine guidance; on 17 September 1583, a month before his enthronement in Canterbury, he wrote, in Calvinist mode, to his friend, Matthew Hutton, at that time Dean of York:

'The burden layed upon me ys verie heavie and great; yet, bycause yt ys God's owne doeing who hath wrogght yt in her Majestie's hart, my trust ys that he wyll also furnish me with gyfts and graces necessarie that I may, without faynting, performe that whereunto he hath so called me.

Yors as hys owne
Jo WIGORN Elect Cant.'

(Overleaf)
Lincoln Cathedral

(Opposite) Ely Cathedral

(Left) This fine timber building in Worcester, now housing Tudor House Museum, would have been known to Whitgift, as it dates from the first half of the sixteenth century

(Below) St Margaret's Church, Laceby, near Grimsby

(Overleaf) Worcester Cathedral

(Below) Another
Worcester landmark
known to Whitgift is
Greyfriars, a timber-
framed house, dating
from 1480, with later
additions

(Opposite) A facsimile
of the page from
Bishop Whitgift's
Register, including the
request for a marriage
licence for William
Shakespeare (Shaxpere)
and Anne Hathaway
(Whateley)

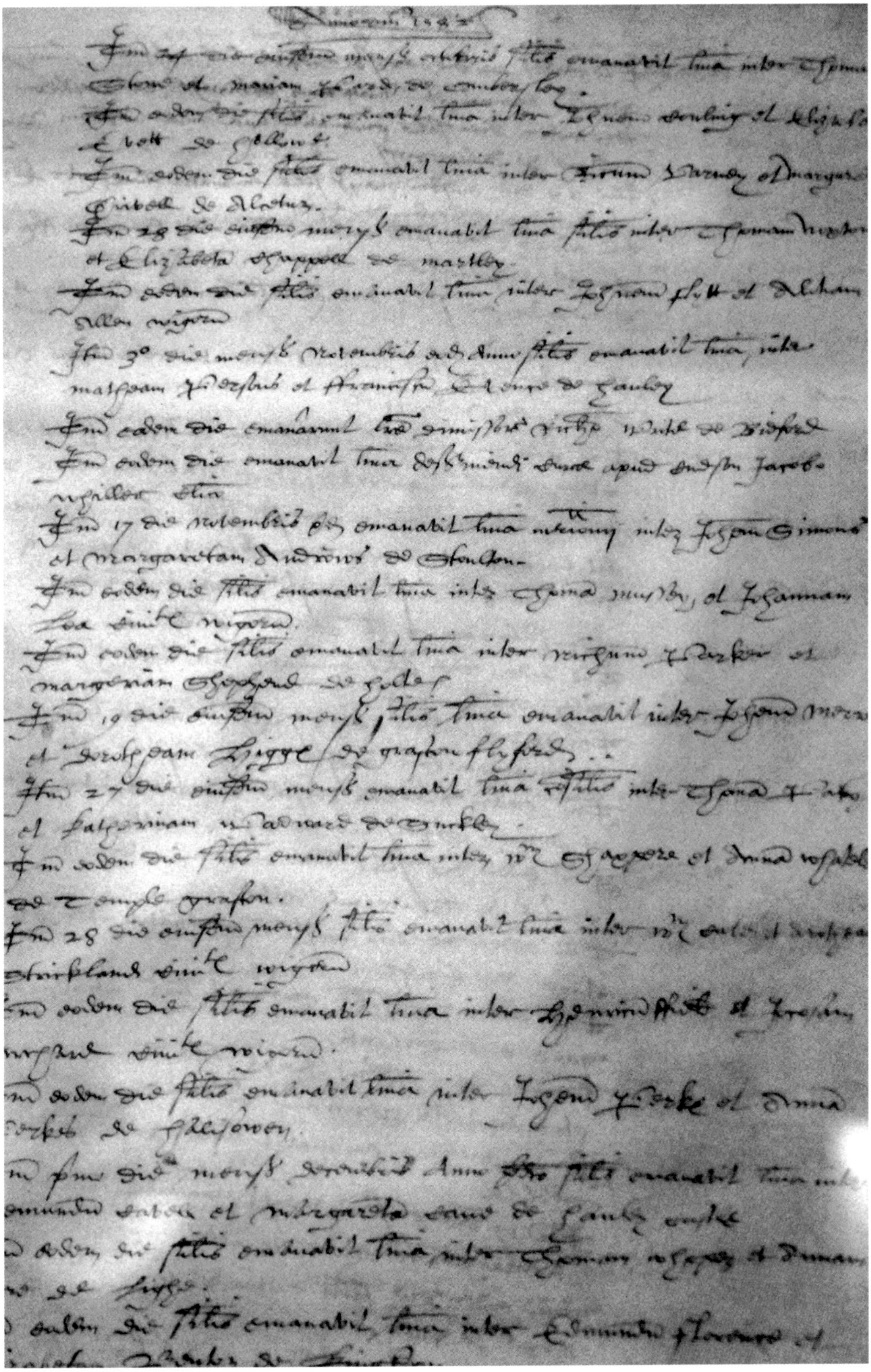

4

Archbishop of Canterbury

Whitgift was enthroned in Canterbury on 23 October 1583. Some of his predecessors had shunned the City almost entirely, barely, if ever, venturing into Kent, choosing rather to live at Lambeth Palace, the Archbishop's London residence, or at another archiepiscopal estate which they found more congenial. Cranmer, Parker and Grindal even sent proxies to their enthronement ceremonies. Whitgift, however, chose to return to Canterbury at regular intervals, as Paule records:

'Every third year he went into Kent (unless great occasions hindred him) where he was so honourably attended upon by his own train (consisting of two hundred persons) and with the gentlemen of the country, that he did sometimes ride into the City of Canterbury, and into other towns, with eight hundred or a thousand horse.'

Whitgift made these triennial progresses from London through Kent to Canterbury, in the manner of the Queen's regular travels through her kingdom, to emphasise to contemporaries his power and status in politics and society, as well as religion. These were consciously ostentatious displays, attracting respect and criticism alike, leading to Whitgift being mocked by Puritan opponents as *'His Canterburiness'*. On one such journey into Kent, in July 1589, when he was followed by a train of clergy, gentlemen and their attendants numbering over 500, Whitgift was accompanied by one hundred of his servants in livery, forty of them wearing cloth of gold.

In Canterbury Cathedral, he encouraged great pomp and ceremony, with robed clergy wearing scarlet hoods, and singing accompanied by organs, cornets and sackbuts. Paule records the reaction of a visitor from Rome who attended a service; he told his companion, Sir Edward Hobby, that he had been led to believe that, after the Reformation, there was no longer any style, substance or structure to ecclesiastical practice in England,

'but that all was pulled down to the ground, and that the People heard their Ministers in woods, and fields, amongst trees, and bruit beasts: but, for his own part, he protested, that (unless it were in the Pope's Chappel) he never saw a more solemn sight, or heard a more heavenly sound.'

Whitgift chose to live in the style of the nobility, at Lambeth Palace, and also in Croydon, at the Archbishop's rural retreat, previously described as the Archbishop's manor house, but increasingly to be termed the Archbishop's Palace. While falling short of the pomp of Hampton Court, when Thomas Wolsey was Archbishop of York and a Cardinal in the Roman Catholic Church, Whitgift enjoyed a comfortable life in his great houses. His household staff at Lambeth numbered well over one hundred, but this was not unprecedented; thirty different categories of servant are listed in the *'Orders and Statutes of Household'*, set out for previous Archbishops, Cranmer and Parker. These posts included a steward; a treasurer; a comptroller; gamators; a clerk of the kitchen; a caterer; a clerk of the spicery; yeoman ushers; butlers of wine and ale; larderers; squilleries; ushers of the hall; a porter; ushers of the chamber; daily waiters in the great chamber; gentlemen ushers; yeomen of the chamber; a carver; a sewer; a cupbearer; grooms of the chamber; a marshal; groom ushers; an almoner; cooks; a chandler; butchers; a master of the horse; yeomen of the wardrobe; and harbingers. Paule, comptroller in Whitgift's household, stresses the particular mix of generosity, allied with a consciousness of status and dignity, with which Whitgift entertained:

'He had a desire always to keep a great and bountiful house; and so he did, having the same well ordered and governed by his head officers therein, and all things in plentiful manner, both for his own service and entertainment of strangers, according to their several qualities and degrees. He often seated the clergy, nobility, and gentry of his Diocess and neighbourhood. And at Christmas, especially, his gates were always open, and his Hall set twice or thrice over with strangers: upon some chief Festival-days he was served with great solemnity, sometime upon the knee, as well for the upholding of the state that belonged unto his place, as for the better education and practice of his gentleman and attendants in point of service.'

Whitgift was also keen to provide the kind of educational opportunities for young men from poorer families that he had experienced, under his uncle's tutelage, at Wellow Abbey:

'…besides the pains which he took himself…many years with a number of worthy young gentlemen, in reading unto them thrice a day, he took into his house, besides his chaplains, divers of quality to instruct them in the Mathematicks, and other lectures of sundry Arts and Languages; giving them good allowance, and preferments otherwise, as occasion was offered. And besides the many poor scholars, whom he kept in his house till he could provide for them, and prefer them (as he did sundry to good estates) he also maintained divers in the university at his own charge, and gave liberally to them and others of any towardliness, as he heard of their necessity, and wants…his house, for the lectures and scholastical exercises therein performed, might justly be accounted a little Academy'.

Whitgift had the position in society, and the necessary wealth, to entertain the Queen, both at Lambeth Palace and in Croydon, without financial ruin. Paule notes that Elizabeth enjoyed her visits:

'Every year he entertained the Queen at one of his houses, so long as he was Archbishop; and some years twice or thrice; where all things were performed in so seemly an order, that she went thence always exceedingly well pleased. And besides many public and gracious favours done unto him, she would salute him, and bid him farewell by the name of Black Husband; calling also his men her servants, as a token of her good contentment with their attendance and pains.'

One of the reasons the Queen gave for liking her visits to the Archbishop, in the same light-hearted spirit as her description of him as her *'black husband'*, with his dark complexion and his black, clerical dress, was the fact that his household contained a number of tall, young men. Just as on first acquaintance she had toyed with the positive portents of his *'white gift'* name, so the choice of an endearing nickname for her Archbishop was another favourable sign. Whitgift joined other leading figures in being given a name, more or less flattering, by the Queen: Burghley was her *'Spirit'*; Burghley's son, Robert Cecil, was *'Pygmy'*; the Earl of Leicester, her *'Eyes'*; Sir Walter Raleigh, *'Water'*; Sir Christopher Hatton, *'Mouton'*. Whitgift apparently had no stand-out features, except a dark complexion, Paule having given us the only description of his appearance to set alongside a variety of portraits painted during his life:

'He was of a middle stature, of a grave countenance, and brown complexion, black hair and eyes, he wore his beard neither long nor thick. For his small timber, he was of a good quick strength, straight and well shaped in all his limbs, to the habit of his body; which began somewhat to burnish towards his latter years.'

The main focus of Whitgift's policy as Archbishop was clear. He had seen a series of religious settlements attempted, and then fail, during his lifetime, unsettling the State, and causing great suffering for many individuals. He was determined that the Elizabethan Settlement would be the enduring one; helping to ensure this outcome peacefully was to prove his most significant achievement. One of his first acts in London was to preach a sermon, at St Paul's Cross, on 17 November 1583, to mark the twenty-fifth anniversary of the Queen's accession. Whitgift strongly emphasised the importance of the Queen's position as Head of the Church, and of accepting obedience to due authority. As ever, his text was chosen with care, on this occasion from Titus, Chapter 3, *'warne them to be subject to rule and power, to obey magistrates'*. He was totally committed to the Settlement of 1559: to the new Prayer Book and the Act of Uniformity, establishing a standard form of worship for the Church and insisting on compulsory church attendance; to the Act of Supremacy, confirming the Queen as the Supreme Governor of the Church; and to the Thirty-Nine Articles, which had followed, in 1563, setting out the distinct beliefs of the new national Church, to which clergy must adhere.

Faced with the feebleness, and sequestration, of Grindal, the Privy Council had taken on many of the powers that would have been exercised by the Archbishop; it was immediately evident that Whitgift would seek to wrest back authority, and provide strong leadership in pursuit of the Queen's cherished conformity. His first move was to require subscription to three particular Articles, setting out specific points of belief: in the Queen's supremacy, in the use of the 1559 Prayer Book, and of no other, and in the fact that the policy enacted was *'agreeable to the word of God'*. Anyone failing to accept these points would lose the right to preach. In the face of sustained pressure, orchestrated by Whitgift, most clergymen chose to subscribe. However, while the proportion of ministers suspended nationally was small, it was significant in several particular counties, with large numbers of suspensions in the eastern counties of Lincolnshire, Norfolk, Suffolk and Essex; many petitioned the Commons seeking redress.

Whitgift tightened the procedures and punishments affecting recusants. He also took powers, in his first year in post, to enable him to act widely, in all Dioceses of the Church, rather than simply in the See of Canterbury, to fine or imprison those who breached the rules governing the Church, and to seek out unlawful books. In 1584, Puritan ministers were the main target; twenty-four specific Articles were published, and all clergymen were required to subscribe, to answer any questions put by ecclesiastical judges, on oath, or, if they refused, face prosecution in the Court of High Commission. In implementing these policies, as they evolved over the subsequent decade, Whitgift enjoyed the benefit of having an able assistant; one of his first acts, on taking up his post in 1583, was to install his friend from Worcester, the lawyer Richard Cosin, as Vicar General of the

Diocese of Canterbury. Cosin was later appointed Dean of the Arches, and served as one of the Judges in the Court of High Commission, which was used to enforce conformity. Whitgift also had the advantage of the assistance of John Boys, the leading ecclesiastical lawyer in Kent, who brought a wealth of experience, serving as Steward of the Liberties of Canterbury to five Archbishops, from Matthew Parker through to George Abbot. Like Cosin, Boys was also a Member of Parliament, and provided a supportive presence for Whitgift when matters affecting the interests of the Church were debated, or considered by various commissions.

Whitgift repeatedly stated that, in all he did, he was acting on the Queen's own direct instructions, and that it was the power of the royal prerogative, backed-up by the Church courts, that gave his actions legitimacy, not the authority of his own office. Whitgift had very little patience with those who would not do as the Queen required, and conform; he described members of a delegation from Kent as 'babes', 'princocks', and 'unlearned sots'. He rounded on one individual with 'thou boy, beardless boy, yesterday bird, new out of shell'. Throughout his life, he found youthful opponents by far the most irritating, and the most likely to break his formidable patience. It was therefore typical that, in 1584, in the face of a hostile parliamentary petition, Whitgift should have expressed the hope that he and his fellow Bishops might be shown more respect, 'for that some of them were preachers when many of the House of Commons had been in their cradles'.

Whitgift was confident in the strength of his position, even when dealing with Burghley, the most powerful man in the Queen's government. The relationship between the two men was a complex one. Burghley had been swift to spot Whitgift's talent, and to encourage the Queen to promote him; however, Burghley often found Whitgift's insistence on conformity too rigid for his own taste. Paule describes Burghley as Whitgift's firm and constant friend, but the reality was a little different, and there was often a tetchiness between them, and divergences of opinion, which peaked periodically.

A fascinating and lengthy exchange of correspondence, in July 1584, during Whitgift's first year in office, illustrates the tension that could well-up between the two men, despite the fact that they were in agreement on most key issues. When Burghley sought to influence Whitgift's use of his powers of patronage, Whitgift tartly rebuffed him, leaving Burghley to complain:

'I did recommend unto your Graces favour two Ministers, Curates of Cambridgeshire, to be favourably heard; and your Grace wrote to me, they were contentious, seditious, and persons vagrant…'

Nettled by Whitgift's refusal to follow his recommendations, Burghley tried to take the Archbishop to task over the manner in which he was proceeding against the

Puritans, and the apparent ruthlessness with which he was insisting on conformity to his twenty-four Articles:

'now, my good Lord, by chance, I am come to the sight of an instrument of twenty-four articles of great length and curiosity, formed in a Romish style, to examine all manner of ministers in this time, without distinction of persons…Which I have read, and find so curiously penned, so full of branches and circumstances, as I think the Inquisitors of Spain use not so many questions to comprehend and to trap their preyes…Now, my good Lord, bear with my scribbling…I desire the peace of the Church. I desire concord and unity in the exercise of religion. I favour no sensual and wilful recusants. But I conclude, that. According to my simple judgment, this kind of proceeding is too much savouring of the Romish inquisition: and is rather a device to seek for offenders, than to reform any'.

Whitgift, while appreciating the power that Burghley wielded, knew that he had the full support of the Queen in implementing his religious policy, and the ready access he enjoyed to the privy chamber, her private apartment, enabled him to plead his causes. He was confident that, because he was acting at the Queen's bidding, he would have enough allies to have the upper hand in the Privy Council on religious matters. He did not like the repeated references to Rome, in Burghley's letter, or to his actions being reminiscent of the Spanish Inquisition. He wrote back to Burghley, lecturing the Lord Treasurer, in a similar manner to the style in which Burghley had chided him:

'In the verie beginning of this action, and so from tyme to tyme, I have made your Lordship acquainted with all my doings…I wold not towch anie for not subscribing onelie, but for breach of order in celebrating divine service, administering sacraments, and executing other ecclesiastical functions, according to their phansies, and not according to the forme by law prescribed…

I know your Lordship desireth the peace of the Church; but how is it possible to be procured, (after so long libertie and lack of discipline) if a few persons, so meanlie qualified as the most of them are, shold be countenanced against the whole state of the Clergie of greatest account for learning, stedyness, wisdom, religion and honestie: and open breakers and impugners of the lawes, yong in yeares, prowd in conceate, contentious in disposition, mainteyned against their superiors and governors, seeking to reduce them to order and to obediens?'

Royal support gave Whitgift the confidence to fight his corner with the most powerful man in England. It also enabled him to stand firm in the face of opposition in Parliament, of the kind he encountered in February 1585, when the Queen made her position clear:

'We understand that some of the Nether house have used divers reproachful speeches against you, tending greatly to your dishonour, which we will not suffer; and that they meddle with matters above their capacity, not appertaining unto them, for the which we will call them to account.'

Despite this, Whitgift encountered on-going criticism, in varying forms, from Members of Parliament over the next two decades, as Puritans and reformers probed the quality of the defences, and the will to resist, of their more conservative opponents. Whitgift believed that concessions to particular requests would inevitably lead to demands for others:

'…will they reste for ever here? And yf they will, shall others doe the like?…this is but a colourable dissembled kinde of dealing, to shake firste one or two stones in the buildinge, that the rest may followe'.

Whitgift's authority was further strengthened, in February 1586, when the Queen approved his appointment to the Privy Council, making him the first cleric to serve since Cardinal Pole, in the reign of Mary I. Puritan sympathisers on the Council, including key office-holders such as Sir Francis Knollys, Treasurer of the Household, Sir Walter Mildmay, Chancellor of the Exchequer, and Sir Francis Walsingham, Secretary of State, had reservations about Whitgift. The long-serving Clerk to the Privy Council, Robert Beale, was notably hostile. However, with the death of the Earl of Leicester in 1588, Whitgift was to lose one of his most powerful critics.

In addition to the strength of the royal support that he enjoyed, Whitgift could count, for the most part, on Burghley's support. He also had close allies of his own: the Lord Chancellor, Sir Christopher Hatton; the Attorney General and later Lord Chief Justice, Sir John Popham; the Speaker of the House of Commons and later Lord Keeper, Sir John Puckering; and many others. Whitgift suggested Hatton for the Lord Chancellor's post, in 1587, when his own name was put forward, and, on Hatton's death, in 1591, Whitgift again declined the Lord Chancellorship, despite being the preferred choice of the Queen.

Whitgift was keen to use his powers to try to eradicate weaknesses within the Church. These, in his view, included the appointment of ill-educated ministers, abuses such as non-residence on the part of office holders, and, ironically in the light of his own path to high office, pluralism. On the latter point, he took a balanced view, however, recognising that the income available to a clergyman from a single post was often totally insufficient. He lamented the fact that more than half the 'livings' in England were worth as little as eight to ten pounds annually, exclaiming:

'Who will apply himself to the study of that profession, wherein he cannot have sufficient maintenance? It is absurd. For what man of reason will think that eight pounds yearly is able to maintain a learned Divine? When as every skull in a kitchen, and groom of a stable, is better provided for?'

He believed it was of the utmost importance to improve the quality of the ministers working in each Diocese, by raising their level of education; a majority was still non-graduate. Whitgift's 1586 Articles, issued from Lambeth, were exceptionally detailed, for once fully deserving the 'schoolmasterly' tag. They set out how a more learned clergy would be achieved:

'Every Minister…shal, before th 2d day of February next, provide a Bible, and Bullinger's Decads (Decades, a book containing fifty godly and learned sermons) *in Latin or English, and a paper-book. And shall every day read over one chapter of the holy Scriptures; and note the principal contents thereof briefly in his paper-book. And shal every week read over one sermon in the said Decads; and note likewise the chief matters therein…And shal once in every quarter… shew his said notes to some preacher neer adjoining, to be assigned for that purpose.'*

To ensure the development of a more educated clergy, those in authority were required to appoint *'certain grave and learned preachers'* who would oversee cluster groups of six or seven less experienced men. In the parishes least well provided for, the Bishop, Archdeacon or other Ordinary (officer of the Church) must see to it

'that there may be in every such parish one sermon at the least every quarter. And the parties charged with the cure of the said parish, shal bear the charges of the dinner, and horse meat of the said preacher'.

Whitgift later claimed that the improvement in the educational standard of the clergy was very marked during his time as Archbishop.

The respect in which he was widely held enabled Whitgift to use the conciliatory skills that he had demonstrated when Bishop of Worcester. When a dispute developed, in York, between Matthew Hutton, as Dean, and Edwin Sandys, as Archbishop, Whitgift urged reconciliation, and sought to make the peace between the two men. He wrote to Hutton, while staying in Croydon, on 23 August 1586:

'For my owne parte, I wish you both so well, that, to make you frendes and to reconcile you together, I would bee content, yf it so pleased her Majesty, to ryde from Croydon to York, yea to Barwick, or fyve tymes furder'.

(Above) Lambeth Palace, much as it would have appeared in the late sixteenth century; the watercolour by Edward Blore, in 1828, predates the extensive remodelling of the Palace

(Left) Canterbury Cathedral

(Opposite) William Cecil, 1st Baron Burghley, painted circa 1572 by an unknown artist

*(Left) Clerical
vestments from the
sixteenth century are
rare; this example of
a mitre is probably
French, and dates from
1592*

*(Opposite) Robert
Devereux, 2nd Earl of
Essex, painted circa
1596 by an unknown
artist*

5
Defender of Church and State

Even with the buttress of royal support, Whitgift's position, as chief defender of the Elizabethan religious settlement, was far from impregnable, and, in the late 1580s, he was to encounter a new and dangerous opposition to his policies, one that took all his strength of character, and all the powers at his disposal, to overcome. Virulent attacks on the Elizabethan Church, and criticism, often highly personal in nature, of certain Bishops, and, in particular, of Whitgift as Archbishop, began to appear in a series of tracts and pamphlets. One of the first of these was John Penry's *A Treatise containing the Aequity of an Humble Supplication*, published in 1587. Penry was a Welsh cleric, a graduate of Peterhouse, Cambridge, one of a younger generation of Puritans. Penry's message, wrapped up in a vast array of biblical quotations and justifications, was straightforward. He argued that the spiritual leaders of the English Church were failing Wales, and allowing *'idolatry and superstition'*, to persist:

'I see the spirituall miserie wherein we now [live] in the Country of Wales, for want of the preaching of the Gospel…the lamentable and wofull estate of us your poore subjects, and brethren, which live at this day altogither without the knowledge of a saving God, because we have not teaching Ministers among us'.

As a large part of the cause of this state of affairs, Penry identified *'non-residences, impropriate livinges, swarmes of ungodly ministers, the insolent, and tyrannicall proceedings of some, joined with pomp too too unreasonable, to keep out a learned and godlie ministerie'.*

If Welsh-speaking ministers could not be found, Penry argued, at least good English-speaking preachers should be provided:

'why can we not have preaching in our owne toung? Because the minister is not able to utter his mind in welsh…Admit we cannot have welsh preachers, yet let us not bee without English where it is understood. There is never a market towne in Wales where English is not as rife as welsh… on the Sea-side they all understand English…upon the marches, they all speake English'.

Whitgift was outraged at what he saw as the deep unfairness and ingratitude of Penry's criticism. Rooting out ignorant, sub-standard clergy, and those who neglected their duties, had been one of his main goals. He felt that he had made major improvements in Wales, while Bishop of Worcester and during his time as Vice President of the Council of Wales and the Marches. Whitgift had also given strong personal support to the use of the Welsh language, encouraging the Welsh scholar, and former Cambridge theologian, William Morgan, in his work on producing the first Welsh Bible, with translations of both the Old and the New Testaments. This had also been an anti-Catholic move, at a time when the threat of a Spanish invasion was building, and Catholic observance persisted in Wales. Whitgift's response to Penry's actions was therefore choleric in the extreme. Copies of Penry's publication were seized, and he was arrested, and brought before the Court of High Commission. Whitgift chose to preside, frequently addressing Penry, who was in his mid-twenties, in derogatory fashion, as *'lewd boy'*. It was the beginning of five years of an unhappy amalgam of persecution and prosecution. Penry could only rail, in his letter *To My Beloved Wife Helena Penry*, subsequently published, at

'the bad and injurious dealing of the Archbishop of Canterbury…I am tossed from post to piller, and permitted to have no assurance of quiet abode'.

The severity of Whitgift's response had the reverse of the desired effect. The attacks on him, and on the Elizabethan Church, were stepped up significantly, in the following year, with the appearance of the first of a series of anonymous pamphlets. The author, or authors, of each of these generally assumed the name Martin Marprelate. The involvement of Penry, in the production of these publications, was strongly suspected, but never proved. Some others thought to have been implicated, such as Job Throckmorton, a Member of Parliament, evaded prosecution. The Martin Marprelate pamphlets focused on the usual Puritan grievances of government by bishops, and the abuses which were held to result from it. The writing was highly satirical and full of witticisms. Whitgift bore the brunt of the attacks. He was described as the *'Beelzebub of Canterbury'*, the *'Canterbury Caiphas'*, *'a monstrous anti-Christ'*, *'the Pope of Lambeth'*, frequently mocked as *'His Canterburiness'*, ridiculed for his displays of wealth and splendour: *'Is seven-score horse nothing, thinkest thou, to be in the train of an English priest?'* Even the strong criticism directed at married bishops, for diverting ecclesiastical revenues for the benefit of their wives and children, was turned against Whitgift:

'To what end else is John of Cant unmarried, but to provide for the bishops' children who shall be poorly left?'

The character assassination was relentless, in pamphlet after pamphlet:

'He [Whitgift] accounteth the preaching of the word an heresy, and doth mortally abhor and persecute it. He will do against law, against God, and against his own conscience, rather than the heresy of preaching should prevail…He is king of pride – he is Lucifer…Concerning pride, some Popes may be inferior to our Bishops: as, for ill-sample, his Canterburiness. A good ill-sample. I will not say his Grace is an infidel; neither yet swear that he is much better. Popery maintaineth the crown of Canterbury. A Paltrypolitan, the Pope of Lambeth, are titles agreeable to his function.'

Many Bishops were criticised, including, for example, Thomas Cooper, Bishop of Winchester, who was the butt of the satirical publication *'Hay, Any Work for a Cooper?'*, but Whitgift was the object of the greatest scorn.

The jibes targeting the Archbishop, and his leadership of the Church, did little to mask the fact that this was, in reality, a sustained campaign against the Elizabethan Settlement itself. Whitgift decided to meet the Martin Marprelate authors head-on, 'to fight fire with fire'. In a fascinating and bold move, aimed at wrong-footing his critics, Whitgift employed several of the leading poets, satirists, playwrights and 'wits' of the day, to respond in kind. These anti-Martinist writers included Thomas Nashe, who wrote a series of books and pamphlets, such as *'An Almond for a Parrat'*, and *'A Myrror for Martinists'*, and John Lyly, who included this witty, anti-Martinist passage in his *'Pappe with an Hatchet'*:

'There is small difference between swallows and Martins, either in shape or nature, save only that the Martins have a more beetle head; they both breed in churches and, having fledged their young ones, leave nothing behind them but dirt. Unworthy to come into the church-

porch or to be nourished under any good man's eaves, that gnaw the bowels in which they were bred, and defile the place in which they were engendered.'

The Martin tracts had first appeared in 1588, the year of the Armada, when it was Catholic Spain, rather than the Puritan enemy within, that was seen as the greatest threat to national security and the national Church. But division in religion could be dangerously weakening in the face of such a severe international threat; the crack-down on those believed to be behind the Martin tracts was therefore sustained and merciless, a matter more of state policy than mere personal vendetta. Whitgift used the powers of the Courts of High Commission and the Star Chamber to the full. The Queen's notorious Secretary of State, Sir Francis Walsingham, lent his network of spies and informers to the cause; torture was sanctioned, to try to exact confessions from the suspected authors, as was detention, without trial, in Newgate prison.

In an atmosphere of greatly-heightened tension, with substantial threats perceived to Church and State, a series of prosecutions was mounted, against the authors of publications deemed seditious or libellous. How closely implicated some of these men were in the production of the Martin publications is often unclear. John Udall, one of the first to face trial, was a Puritan pamphleteer, lecturing in Kingston upon Thames. Having graduated from Trinity College, Cambridge, just after Whitgift had completed his term as Master, Udall had many powerful allies in the academic world, and in society, including the Earl of Huntingdon, and the Earl of Essex, and he had preached before James VI in Scotland. But he was an associate of Penry, and, in his publication, *A Demonstration of Discipline*, circulated in 1588, he had attacked *'the supposed governors of the church of England, the archbishops, lord-bishops, archdeacons and the rest of that order'*. He was tried at the Surrey Assizes in Croydon, and died in prison in 1592.

The culmination of the anti-Martin campaign came in 1593. Penry himself was charged with having *'feloniously devised and written certain words with intent to excite rebellion and insurrection in England,'* in his book entitled *'Reformation, No Enemy'*. He was found guilty and hanged, in especially-brutal fashion, without being allowed any of the usual courtesies, such as a final farewell to his wife and four daughters; Whitgift's was the first signature on Penry's death warrant. To his supporters, Penry was a Welsh martyr. To his opponents, he was a dangerous agitator; for them, he had known the risks he was taking, had persisted in his course despite opportunities to recant, and had therefore met his inevitable fate, given the harsh realities of the politics of religion at the time.

As a consequence of the prosecutions, the more extreme forms of Puritanism were subdued for the remainder of Elizabeth's reign, until they sparked into life, with greater force, during the early decades of the seventeenth century. Whitgift's crushing of Penry was accompanied by the hanging of two Puritans, Henry Barrow and John Greenwood, also in 1593, after a determined campaign against them for their separatist and anti-establishment doctrines, over a period of seven years. Barrow had stirred Whitgift's anger with very personal attacks, describing the Archbishop as

a monster, a miserable compound…he is neither ecclesiastical nor civil, even that second beast spoken of in the Revelation'.

However ill-judged, extreme or poisonous the language, however great the potential dangers to the unity of the Country, these unedifying trials, before the Courts of Church and State, inevitably darkened Whitgift's subsequent reputation, particularly once the crises to which they related had passed. The suffering of a relatively small number of individuals overshadowed the achievement of decades of peace. The prosecutions typified contemporary belief in the end justifying the means, and served to obscure the fact that, by the standards of his time, Whitgift was generally a more tolerant and moderate man than many of his peers. From time to time, however, his temper got the better of him, as men such as Penry, Barrow, or Greenwood discovered to their cost. Barrow described Whitgift's fury at his Second Examination, in November 1587:

'Canterburie [Whitgift], *with a grimme and angrie countenance …* [threatened me with] *yow shalnot prattle here, come at him: I wil make him tel an other tale, yet* (before) *I have done with him.'*

Even the loyal Paule acknowledged the *'choler'* in his master, which could have such severe consequences. It is also possible to discern the strong influence, in the more extreme anti-Puritan actions of this period, of Richard Bancroft, Whitgift's Chaplain, a key ecclesiastical commissioner, and Whitgift's longtime ally, the lawyer, Richard Cosin.

In direct contrast to his time in Worcester, Whitgift was far more active against certain Puritan opponents than against Catholics. The latter seemed the lesser danger to the Elizabethan Settlement, after the execution of Mary, Queen of Scots, in 1587, and the defeat of the Spanish Armada, in 1588. The number of active Catholics had declined; there was also far greater uniformity in formulating national policy on all issues touching on Roman Catholicism, and greater unity within the Privy Council, than on the question of how best to respond to Puritan critics. But there was no certainty of tolerance, even if many Catholics were left undisturbed in their faith. Recusants were regularly brought before Whitgift and his Commissioners, with particular purges, as in 1590. Penalties for recusancy were made tougher in the Parliament of 1593, and, in the period of two and a half decades to the end of Elizabeth's reign, as another stark reminder of the severity of punishments in the sixteenth century, more than fifty Catholic priests were executed.

In the final years of the century, Whitgift found himself caught up in debates within the Church, concerning particular interpretations of Calvinist beliefs, that he would surely have much preferred to see left undisturbed. William Whitaker, a former scholar and subsequently Fellow of Trinity College, Cambridge, while Whitgift had been Master, locked horns, in 1595, with another Cambridge theologian, William Barrett, a Fellow of Caius College; others, including, principally, Peter Baro, Lady Margaret Professor of Divinity, joined in. At first, this seemed likely to remain a Cambridge dispute, with Calvinist and anti-Calvinist proclamations and interpretations, from various pulpits, on the nature of predestination, free will and God-given grace. Whitgift tried to exert his authority to decide such matters, writing to the Heads of Colleges:

'It is a most vain conceit to think that you have authority in matters of controversy to judge what is agreeable to the doctrine of the Church of England and what is not... how far my authority under her highness reacheth ...I hope you will not give me occasion to try'.

He had, in fact, good reason to know the limitations of his own authority when faced with a determination, on the part of the Queen, to have her own way. Whitgift had attempted, for example, to intercede with Elizabeth on behalf of Matthew Hutton, now Bishop of Durham, who had reservations about moving to become Archbishop of York. Whitgift had to admit defeat, in a letter to Hutton, on 4 November 1594:

'I have signified to her Highnesse that you are better, in respect of living, now, where you are placed, and that I thought you wold be lothe to remove. She answered that you shal remove, and that you are well able to bere the charges thereof: so that you must prepare yourself thereto, if this resolution hold, as I think it will'.

Despite this clear reminder that royal authority eclipsed his own, overconfidence in his position, and in the royal support which underpinned it, led Whitgift to make a significant mistake. Without securing the Queen's approval in advance, he issued new Lambeth Articles, in November 1595, which had been drafted by Whitaker, nine points of belief that came down firmly in favour of predestination. He set out the doctrine he wished to have adopted as the official line, with a view to ending another, potentially interminable, debate:

'God from eternity has predestined some men to life, and condemned some to death...The number of the predestined is determined and certain and cannot be increased or diminished ...Those not predestined to salvation are inevitably condemned for their sins...It is not in the will or the power of each and every man to be saved.'

Elizabeth was not at all amused; the Archbishop's intervention was seen as dignifying the debate, and the Articles as a whole did not meet with the Queen's approval. Robert Cecil, who had already taken on some of his father's duties, and would become the Queen's leading minister on Burghley's death, wrote to Whitgift, on 5 December 1595, that the Queen, having now seen the Lambeth Articles, insisted on them being withdrawn:

'she misliked much that any allowance had been given by his Grace and the rest, of any such points to be disputed: being a matter tender and dangerous to weak and ignorant minds. And thereupon she required his Grace to suspend them.'

The special relationship between Elizabeth and her *'black husband'* would get back onto a happier and securer footing in due course, but this was a stern royal rebuff which he had to accept. The only other instance of Whitgift incurring significant royal displeasure at this time resulted from his pleading the cause of his former tutee, the Earl of Essex, during the royal favourite's turbulent relationship with the Queen. Paule remembered that:

'such was the confidence the archbishop had in the earl's loyalty, and his own stedfastness in that friendship which he had formerly professed unto him, that he could not be drawn from being a continual intercessor for him; wherewith her Majesty was so highly displeased, and so sharply rebuked him for the same, that the good old Archbishop came sometimes home much grieved and perplexed.'

Now well into his sixties, Whitgift's health was steadily deteriorating during the mid -to-late 1590s, and he had little choice but to devolve an increasing degree of responsibility onto the man who would in due course replace him as Archbishop, Richard Bancroft. The two men had had a similar rise; both were Cambridge clerics and, to an extent, protégés of Richard Cox, the Bishop of Ely. Like Whitgift before him, Bancroft held a Chaplaincy at Ely and enjoyed the income from the Rectory at Teversham. As Canon of Westminster, a Chaplain to Whitgift's ally, the Lord Chancellor, Sir Christopher Hatton, and subsequently to Whitgift himself, Bancroft had become a key advisor and confidant of the Archbishop during the Martin Marprelate affair. Bancroft was consecrated Bishop of London in May 1597, and increasingly took a lead, on Whitgift's behalf, in the implementation of ecclesiastical policy. With Bancroft's strong support, Whitgift was able to negotiate a path through the final years of Elizabeth's reign with no little skill.

These years at the turn of the century remained difficult ones. On 27 August 1599, Whitgift wrote to Matthew Hutton: *'You cannot but here* (hear) *what alarums we have had, and yet have, of the Spanyerds approaching'*. Even though the prospect of a foreign invasion was generally receding, and the Puritan threat diminishing, these fears were being replaced by concerns over the succession to the Throne. The ageing Virgin Queen declined to name her successor, and there was nervousness in Church and State over any development that might threaten the nation's stability. This atmosphere was reflected in an increasingly-overt use of the powers of censorship, where royal whim, ecclesiastical policy and political expediency converged in an uneasy amalgam. Responsibility for the control of publications, and for the banning and destruction of those deemed offensive, was shared between the Privy Council, the Chancellors of Oxford and Cambridge Universities, the Bishop of London and the Archbishop of Canterbury. In addition, the Company of Stationers had the authority to seize and burn unlicensed books, and the Queen could exercise her prerogative to intervene, without warning, at any time.

The Archbishop had the chief responsibility, and control of the moral compass, so the fact that Whitgift's period in office saw the publication, or performance on the Elizabethan stage, of some of the finest works ever penned in the English language, must stand greatly to his credit. A more ruthless policy of censorship, on the part of the various licensing authorities, in the 1590s, which Whitgift could have orchestrated, would have meant that many, if not all, of the following works would have been cut or obliterated: Sir Philip Sidney's *Arcadia*, Edmund Spenser's *The Faerie Queene*, Christopher Marlowe's *Dr Faustus* and *Tamburlaine*, and a large number of Shakespeare's plays, including *Richard II*, *Richard III*, *Romeo and Juliet*, *Henry IV Parts 1 and 2* and *Henry V*, *A Midsummer Night's Dream*, *Macbeth*, and *Hamlet*. Occasionally, royal patience, severely tested by certain plays, for example Shakespeare's *Richard II*, with its focus on an unpopular ruler and the dangers of an uncertain succession, was pushed beyond its limits. The clearest example of this came in June 1599, with the infamous 'Bishops' Ban' or 'Bishops' Bonfire', which followed a decree from Whitgift *that no satires or epigrams be printed hereafter*'. In fact, the ban is now seen as a short-lived attempt to rein in a number of publications, including satirical and erotic works, such as Marlowe's translation of Ovid's *Elegies*, perhaps at the Queen's direction, to emphasise who was ultimately in control of the publication process. Whitgift himself had only intermittently tolerated Marlowe's works, and played a significant part in bringing him before the Privy Council in 1593, to answer charges of blasphemy. The books now burnt, in 1599, included all of Thomas Nashe's writings, an ironic turn of fate given that Whitgift had been his patron, employing him during the Martin Marprelate affair, and commissioning one of Nashe's finest works, *'Summer's Last Will and Testament'*, for a royal première at his Palace in Croydon.

Shakespeare, however, rather than showing any gratitude to Whitgift, for escaping censorship of his work, chose to side with the victims of the Archbishop's censorship, as A Jack and FHG Percy have pointed out in their studies. The Second Quarto version of *Hamlet* was published soon after Whitgift's death, in 1604, and Shakespeare marked the Archbishop's demise by inserting additional lines into one of the Ghost's speeches, in the new version of his play; ostensibly directed solely at Hamlet's uncle, Claudius, the lines carried a barely-veiled, personal attack on Whitgift:

'Ay, that incestuous, that adulterate beast,
With witchcraft of his wit, with traitorous gifts, -
O wicked wit and gifts, that have the power
So to seduce…
…a wretch whose natural gifts were poor
To those of mine!'

The emphatic repetition of 'wit' and 'gifts', unusually laboured for Shakespeare, ensured that contemporary audiences would not miss his meaning.

Another of the finest writers of the age, Edmund Spenser, like Whitgift a former student at Pembroke College, Cambridge, took a totally opposite stance to that of Shakespeare. In his great allegorical work, *The Faerie Queene*, written in the 1590s, there is a warm, cameo portrait of Whitgift, as a black pilgrim, or *'palmer'*, with exceptional, magical powers for good:

'A comely palmer, clad in black attire,
Of ripest yeares, and heares all hoarie gray,
That with a staffe his feeble steps did stire,
Least his long way his aged limbs should tire:
And if by looks one may the mind aread,
He seemd to be a sage and sober syre…
The palmer over them his staffe upheld,
His mighty staffe, that could all charmes defeat…
Such wondrous power did in that staffe appeare,
All monsters to subdew to him that did it beare.'

Spenser also credits Whitgift with a very positive influence over the Earl of Essex. The Earl is portrayed by Spenser as Sir Guyon in the poem, and Whitgift, the *'blacke palmer'*, keeps him on the 'straight and narrow':

'With that blacke palmer, his [Essex's] most trusty guide;
Who suffred not his wandering feete to slide.
But when strong passion or weak fleshlinesse
Would from the right way seeke to draw him wide,
He would through temperaunce and stedfastnesse
Teach him the weal to strengthen, and the strong suppresse'.

Whitgift stayed loyal to his former tutee during all the setbacks which Essex encountered, and the cooling of the Earl's relationship with the Queen. The Archbishop did not waver in his support, and, on the death of Lord Burghley, in 1598, when Essex was elected Chancellor of Cambridge University, Whitgift wrote to the Vice-Chancellor:

'knowing the disposition of the Earl of Essex towards learning and learned men I do not think any man in England so fit for that office as he is'.

Suddenly, in February 1601, there came a moment of crisis. Increasingly frustrated and angered, shut out from access to the Queen, and deprived of the income he had previously enjoyed from the trade in sweet wines, Essex fortified his London residence, Essex House, in the Strand. He then tried to march, with his armed supporters, to force an audience with Elizabeth. Ironically, it fell to Whitgift to play a key role in snuffing out the danger, his loyalty to the Queen readily surmounting that to his friend. Paule, who would often have seen the two men together, claimed that he had warned his master that it would end badly with Essex, but that he could not get Whitgift to believe it. Paule witnessed the events of the tragedy unfold:

'The Archbishop being that Sunday morning at the Court…hastened home without any attendant, and commanded as many men as he then had in the house to be presently armed, and sent them over unto the Court… There were immediately presented unto him threescore men well armed, and appointed, who with a message from the Archbishop shewed themselves before the Court, of whose arrival there Master secretary Cecill, with the rest of the Lords of the Council, were right glad, and said he was a most worthy Prelate. They…were the first that entred into the gates of Essex-house; and…made good the place until the Earl yielded himself, and was by the Lord Admiral brought to Lambeth-house, where he remained an hour or two, and was from thence conveyed to the Tower.'

Whitgift kept forty armed horsemen on standby during the afternoon:

'The next morning he sent a gentleman to know how the Queen did, and how she rested all night. To whom she made answer, that she rested and slept the better for his care the day before.'

Essex was ruined, found guilty of treason, and executed. Whitgift was restored to royal favour:

'When Her Majesty understood that her own recommendation of the Earl had wrought that good opinion of him in the Archbishop, and that she now found his readiness for her defence, with horse, and men, and the nearness thereof unto the Court, to stand her at that time in great stead, she began to entertain him in her wonted favour and grace again, and ever after continued her good opinion of him unto her dying day.'

*(Above) Queen
Elizabeth I, by an
unknown artist, circa
1585-90*

*(Opposite) William
Cecil, when Lord
Treasurer and 1st
Baron Burghley, by an
unknown artist*

4.

An Almond for a Parrat,
Or
Cutbert Curry-knaues
Almes.

Fit for the knaue Martin, and the
rest of those impudent Beggers, that
can not be content to stay their stomakes
with a Benefice, but they will needes
breake their fastes with
our Bishops.

Rimarum sum plenus.

Therefore beware (gentle Reader) you
catch not the hicket with laughing.

Imprinted at a Place, not farre from
a Place, by the Assignes of Signior Some body, and
are to be sold at his shoppe in Trouble-knaue
Stræt, at the signe of the
Standish.

(Above) A deed poll, dated 7 December 1602, bearing Whitgift's signature, appointing his attorney, Edward Aylworth, to act for him in respect of property in Crome Hurst, near Croydon

(Right) A letter from Whitgift to John Boys, dated 5 July 1592, also bearing his Jo Cantuar signature

(Opposite) 'An Almond for a Parrat', an anti-Martin Marprelate pamphlet by Thomas Nashe, published circa 1589

(Left) Portrait of Archbishop Whitgift, aged 68, by an unknown artist, from his Hospital

(Below) John Speed's map, from his 'Theatre of the Whole Island of Great Britaine' series, first published in the early seventeenth century, showing Lambeth and Croydon

(Opposite) Portrait of Richard Bancroft, Bishop of London, and later Archbishop of Canterbury, by an unknown artist

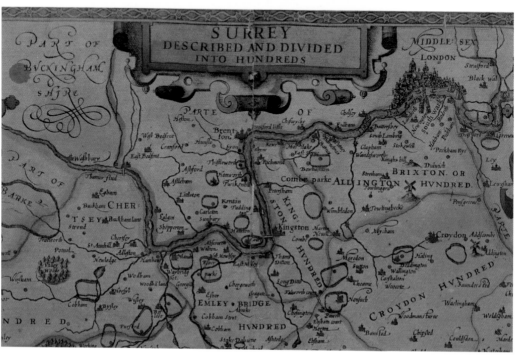

6

Croydon

The Domesday Book of 1086 lists the manor of Croindene (Croydon), with its church, mill, meadow and woodland, as belonging to the See of Canterbury, with Lanfranc, the Archbishop, as Tenant-in-Chief and Lord of the Manor. Croydon was one of a series of manors, stretching from Canterbury to Lambeth, providing convenient points along the journey between them, at which the Archbishop and accompanying retinue could stay. Sadly for his successors, Thomas Cranmer, Archbishop in Henry VIII's reign, had had little option but to give up many of these rural, ecclesiastical residences to the Crown. Henry, with his voracious appetite for monastic and church property, acquired Otford, Knole and Maidstone in 1537, Aldington, Saltwood Castle and Lyminge in 1540, and Charing and Mayfield in 1545. This left the Archbishops with Canterbury itself, Lambeth Palace in London, the Ford and Bekesbourne estates in Kent, and Croydon, remaining in their possession.

Many Archbishops of Canterbury chose to stay for periods of time at their manor house in Croydon, enjoying entertaining there and welcoming the monarch, the earliest recorded royal visit being by Henry III, in 1229. Whitgift himself, while inevitably spending the great majority of his time at Lambeth, close to the Court and the centre of national politics and administration, particularly appreciated opportunities to reside at his Croydon house.

Twenty-first century Croydon is a London Borough, and, with a population now estimated at well over a third of a million, one of the most populous. Two centuries after Whitgift's death, when the first national census was taken in 1801, Croydon had just 1,074 houses, and 5,743 inhabitants. In the late sixteenth century, it was an even smaller town, with perhaps around 2,000 residents, situated on the principal road from London to the Coast and the towns of Portslade and Brighton. Croydon was renowned for its oats, and for the production of charcoal, which led the town to have more than the usual quota of smiths and colliers. Its reputation was picked up in a number of plays and literary allusions in Whitgift's time: John Aldee's play *'Like will to like quod the Devil to the Collier'* has the character Tom Collier of Croydon; another sixteenth-century play is entitled *'Grim the Collier of Croydon'*; and Robert Greene's *'A Quip for an Upstart Courtier'*, of 1592, has the following line: *'Marry, quoth hee that lookt like Lucifer...I am not the divell, but indeed a collier of Croydon.'*

What especially drew Whitgift to Croydon was its quiet, rural beauty. The parkland of Whitgift's estate would have recalled something of the environment he had known at Wellow Abbey, in his childhood. The modern name Croydon, with many older spellings including Croindene, and Crogdaene, is of uncertain derivation; it is thought that it perhaps originally signified 'meandering', or 'crooked valley', or alternatively, 'valley of the crocuses', or 'sheep valley', depending on whether the actual origin is Norse/Danish, Celtic, Anglo-Saxon or Norman/French, a combination, or a corruption. William Camden, the historian and antiquarian of late Elizabethan England, included Croydon in his famous work, *Britannia*:

'The cleare rivulet Wandle...so full of the best trouts...issueth from his head neare Carshalton... while it is yet small, receiveth his first increase by a rill [small stream] *springing at Croidon... which standing under the hills, is very well known, as well for the house of the archbishops of Canterburie, unto whom it hath belonged now this long time, as for charcoles which the townspeople make good chaffer* [trade] *of.'*

Whitgift's residence, together with the parish church of St John the Baptist (now designated Croydon Minster, and rebuilt after a fire in 1867), stood, in the sixteenth century, on an island, surrounded by the River Wandle (now culverted over), and a series of fishponds. It was in a hollow, set down the hill from the High Street, with a large wood providing additional privacy. There was also an adjoining park for hunting, a pursuit in which Whitgift engaged both here, and at another of his houses, Ford Park, in Cressy, Kent.

Opinions differed as to the suitability of this particular place for a house. The Wandle was free-flowing there, close to its springs located in the area later occupied by the Swan and Sugar Loaf public house, but the land around Whitgift's house was low-lying. Henry VII, grandfather of Queen Elizabeth I, clearly liked it, staying there regularly as a guest of Archbishop Warham, during the later years of his reign. Henry VIII, by contrast, disliked the place intensely: *'it standeth lowe, and is reumatike, where I could never be withoute sycknes'*. Perhaps it also brought back uneasy memories of visits to Croydon, and nearby Beddington Park, with their links to both Catherine of Aragon and Anne Boleyn. Edmund Grindal, Whitgift's predecessor as Archbishop, who was to die in Croydon, shared Henry VIII's view, describing it as *'no wholesome house'*. Sir Francis Bacon remembered Whitgift's house as *'an obscure and darke place'*. On a later visit, cited in Garrow's *History of Croydon*, after Archbishop Abbot had lived there for some years, he hardly recognised it:

'Lord Chancellor Bacon riding by that way, asked his man; Whose fair house that was? The man told him it was my Lord of Canterbury's; It is not possible, for his building is environed with wood; It is true, Sir, it was so, but he hath lately cut it down; By my troth, answered Bacon, he hath done very judiciously...he hath expounded and cleared it wonderfully well.'

Whitgift must have turned in his grave. He loved the house, the beauty of the Wandle, the parkland, woods and vineyards. Paule records:

'the Archbishop had ever a great affection to lie at his Mansion house at Croydon, for the sweetness of the place, especially in summertime; whereby also he might sometimes retire himself from the multiplicity of businesses and suitors in the vacations'.

Unlike her father, Queen Elizabeth seems to have much enjoyed her visits to Croydon. She stayed several times as a guest of her first Archbishop, Parker, and, as well as regularly visiting Whitgift at Lambeth Palace, she was a frequent guest in Croydon, sometimes more than once a year. The Queen also stayed with Whitgift's neighbours, Sir Francis Carew at Beddington, or Charles Howard, 1st Earl of Nottingham, at Haling Park. No record has survived of the majority of the royal visits to the Archbishop's Palace in Croydon, to which Paule refers, apart from an occasional, often tantalizing mention in the historical record.

The historian, Marion Colthorpe, researched the Queen's visits to the horse races in Croydon, and unearthed some fascinating material, in an article published by the Surrey Archaeological Society. Elizabeth appears to have attended the Croydon horse races on several occasions in the second half of the 1580s. In 1585, having already visited Croydon at the beginning of April, she returned, for a stay lasting from 28 April to 3 May. Payment was made

'To fraunces Coote one of thordenarye gentlemen ushers of her majesties Chamber for thallowance of him selfe, one yeoman usher, iii yeoman and ii gromes of the chamber, ii

gromes of the wardrobe and i grome porter for makinge ready for her majestie the Bishoppes house at Croydon'.

In 1586, expenditure was incurred on making and transporting to Croydon

'a newe frame with a flower in it for the Quenes Majestie, ye noblemen, and ladies to stande in, to see the race runne with horsses nere Croydon'.

In 1588, work is again recorded in

'Croydon [at] *the lorde Archbishoppe of Canterbury his Graces house...*[preparing] *A Standinge there for her Majestie to see the horsrace runne'*.

The actual race-day appears to have been 1 May each year. The Archbishop's attendance, with his royal guest at the Croydon races, before returning to his Palace, may be presumed, but there is no record to confirm it. These were major social occasions for Whitgift and for Croydon; during her 1587 visit, for example, the Queen also took the opportunity, during a stay with Whitgift, to appoint his friend, Sir Christopher Hatton, to be her new Lord Chancellor.

Perhaps the most special of the visits made by the Queen to her Archbishop in Croydon would have been the one in the late summer of 1592. The Plague had been prevalent in London, and many had left the City, the Queen included. She departed on a royal progress in August, continuing through September with visits to a number of towns and country houses in Surrey, including Farnham, Godalming, and Nonsuch Palace, where Ben Jonson's *Every Man his Humor* was performed, before arriving at Whitgift's Palace. The Queen's love of masques, plays, and similar entertainments was frequently indulged by her wealthier subjects, and Whitgift was not to be found wanting. He had commissioned Thomas Nashe, whom he had previously employed during the Martin Marprelate affair, to write a new piece, *Summer's Last Will and Testament*, described as '[not a masque] *'tis no play neither, but a shew'*, especially for the Queen's visit.

Fortunately, the text of the *'shew'* has survived, published in 1600. The characters include the Seasons, Harvest, Bacchus, Christmas, and a Chorus; commentary on the action comes from a character taking the name of Henry VIII's court fool, Will Summer (or Sommers), who had still been at Court when Elizabeth came to the Throne. Some parts in the show would, most likely, following contemporary practice in other performances before the Queen, have been taken by a troupe of child actors, perhaps the Children of the Chapels Royal. The child actors and singers, again according to custom, would have been joined by members of Whitgift's household, with the production staged in his Great Hall; the actors playing the hobby-horse are warned, at one point, *'goe not too fast, for feare of wearing out my Lords tyle-stones with your hob-nayles'*. When Summer first appears, his lines have been carefully penned to flatter 'Eliza', Whitgift's Guest of Honour:

'What pleasure alway lasts? No joy endures:
Summer I was, I am not as I was;
Harvest and age have whit'ned my greene head:
On Autumne now and Winter must I leane.
Needs must he fall, whom none but foes uphold.
Thus must the happiest man have his blacke day:
…This month have I layne languishing abed,
Looking eche houre to yeeld my life, and throne;
And dyde I had indeed unto the earth
But that Eliza Englands beauteous Queene,
On whom all seasons prosperously attend,
Forbad the execution of my fate
Untill her joyful progresse was expirid.
For her doth Summer live, and linger here…[in Croydon]*'*

Summer's Last Will and Testament contains various references and allusions to Croydon and the surrounding area. Summer states *'I give…My pleasant open ayre and fragrant smels/To Croyden and the grounds abutting round'*, and dancers are introduced to the audience as the *'finest set of morris-daunters that is betweene this* [Croydon] *and Stretham'*. The reference is an interesting one; Whitgift showed, on a number of occasions, his willingness to allow traditional dancing and associated customs, including early in his term as Archbishop, when he removed prohibitions on Whitsun ales and morris dancing imposed by his predecessor, Grindal.

Nashe knew just where the boundaries of his art lay, the witticisms with which to amuse the Queen, to anticipate her return, and to poke fun at Whitgift, her host, and his *'lowe built house'*.

And finally, O words, now clense your course,
Unto Eliza that most sacred Dame,
Whom none but Saints and Angels ought to name;
All my faire dayes remaining, I bequeath
To waite upon her till she be returnd.
…Autumne hath all the Summers fruitefull treasure,

Gone is our sport, fled is poore Croydens pleasure:
Short dayes, sharpe dayes, long nights come on a pace,
…This lowe built house, will bring us to our ends.
From winter, plague & pestilence, good Lord deliver us.

Nashe was permitted to mock the Archbishop's deeply-held beliefs: *'I promise you truely, I was almost asleep, I thought I had bene at a Sermon'*. Even Whitgift's commitment to academia did not escape attention. With the Queen a guest in his own home, he allows Nashe to pour scorn on the education and scholarship that he so valued:

'Yong men, yong boyes, beware of Schoolemasters, They will infect you, marre you, bleare your eyes…Latin it was the speech of infidels…Out upon it, who would be a Scholler? not I, I promise you: my minde always gave me, this learning was such a filthy thing, which made me hate it so as I did: when I should have beene at schoole, construing Batte, mi fili, mi fili, mi Batte, I was close under a hedge, or under a barne wall, playing at spanne Counter, or Jacke in a boxe: my master beat me, my father beat me, my mother gave me bread and butter, yee all this would not make me a squitter-booke…Here before all this companie, I professe my selfe on open enemy to Inke and paper…Nownes and Pronounes, I pronounce you as traitors to boyes buttockes, Syntaxis and Prosodia, you are tormenters of wit, & good for nothing but to get a school master two pence a weeke. Hang copies, flye out phrase books, let pennes be turnd to picktooths: bowles, cards & dice, you are the true liberal sciences. I'll nere be Goose-quill, gentlemen, while I live.'

Nashe's brilliance sheds light on the character of his patron, at one of the high points of his social life; Whitgift, spectator and host, is confirmed as a confident man, more relaxed and far more broad-minded than the pedant caricatured by his opponents.

In 1596, Whitgift wrote the will that was to bind his name down the centuries to Croydon. Amongst its provisions, he made bequests to relatives, and provided for certain possessions, particularly books from his library, to go to Lambeth Palace, and to academic institutions with which he had been associated. In addition, he decided to leave a substantial legacy to Croydon. He set out his intention to build a hospital for elderly residents, and a new school. Just over a decade earlier, in 1584, Whitgift had re-founded Eastbridge Hospital in Canterbury, which had a linked school, to provide accommodation for ten elderly poor people of the City, and support to a further ten: his reforms were confirmed in an Act of Parliament. He had also revised the statutes for the Hospitals of St John and St Nicholas, Harbledown, in Canterbury, and had served as one of the first Governors of Sir John Hawkins Hospital, founded in Chatham, in 1594. Following a similar pattern to the Eastbridge Foundation, his Croydon Foundation was established, in 1596, by Act of Parliament. The Bishop of London, the Bishop of Bath and Wells, and George Paule, from his own household, were amongst the witnesses to Whitgift's signature on the Charter of Incorporation. Whitgift had chosen a healthier site, above his own Palace, on higher ground, where the Checquer Inn stood; it was purchased for £200 in February 1595, together with other land and properties in Croydon, totalling thirteen acres, to form part of his Foundation's endowment. An adjoining house was purchased for £30, followed by another Inn, the Swan, a little further to the north, with four acres of land, for £80. A building and an acre and a half of land, called Staycross, adjoining the Checquer Inn, was purchased for £80, in October 1596, to provide a suitable site for his new school.

Even in setting up his Foundation, Whitgift could not escape controversy, with some suggesting that he was merely appeasing his conscience, the scale of his benefaction revealing the great wealth he had extracted from his post. He responded to his critics in typically direct and detailed fashion:

'The archbishopric is no better to me than it was to my late predecessors; who died not very wealthy, for anything I can learn: and I hope I bestow it as well as they did. But whosoever saith that this archbishopric is yearly worth £6000, or worth anyway, in ordinaries or extraordinaries, £3000, must answer to God at the least for vain speeches, that I term them no worse. And yet out of that which any way I receive, there goeth in annuities, pensions, subsidies, and other duties to Her Majesty, £800 at the least. And then what remaineth is soon known. And other ways I receive not one penny. The land which I had before mine advancement, and which I have purchased since, my brethren have, those excepted which I have bestowed upon mine hospital.'

Whitgift's own accounts for 1587 show his income to have been £2,215. He even felt obliged to set out what he had given to family members:

'One farm, called Chamberlayns, in Clavering, in the County of Essex. For my brother, William Whitgift. Which cost me £470.
Toward the purchasing of a piece of land in Kent, for my brother George Whitgift. I gave to him £400.
One house in Shorne in Kent, with two acres of ground, which cost me £100 and the reversion of a lease.
Two tenements in Shorne, and some three acres belonging which cost me £121.2s. Rent £8.10s.
One cottage and fifty acres of marsh land in Kent, for my nephew John Whitgift, which cost £432. Rent £24.'

Whitgift was to spend significantly more on constructing and endowing his new hospital and school than he had on his relatives. A further eighty-seven acres was purchased to the east, near Stroud Green, together with a number of farms at Woodside, Shirley and Addiscombe, for the large sum of £1,400. He continued to purchase additional properties, in the remaining years before his death, notably the three hundred and forty acres of the Manor of Croham, for £740.

The Vicar of Croydon, Samuel Fynche, was charged with keeping a close eye on the building works for the Hospital, the design of which was intended to mimic that of a Cambridge college. Whitgift himself took a strong interest in the work, which commenced in January 1596, and took just over three years to complete. He personally laid two corner-stones, on 22 March 1596, and was regularly updated, in great detail by Fynche, on the progress being made:

'The yarde is all defenced in, strong and safe. This day we made an end in pulling down [the old inn]. *Nowe we take mortar-makinge in hand, clensing and levellinge the grounde; and by Monday come sevennighte…we shall be readye for the foundacon and bricklayer. Weeks the bricklayer hath been at your brick-clamps* (an old method of brick construction in individual, free-standing kilns)*, and he commends them for very good. We have our sande from Dubbers* (Duppas) *Hill…Blease* [the bricklayer] *hath begune the grounde worke nexte the highway leadinge to London; and finding that grounde made and false, digged the trench alonge the door unto some four foote deepe, and three foote wide…and findinge firme grounde, they have filled up that trenche with great flinte and small stone, and brickbats and rubbishe not confusedly, but orderlye layed in, and rammed stronglye, course upon course, strong and sure…Four loads of flinte, which come to ten shillings, will save one thousand of bricks at sixteen shillings…'*

In addition to the use of local sand, much of the timber was obtained from Whitgift's own park, and from Lingfield in Surrey. Fynche knew Whitgift's desire for attention to detail in every aspect of the work. He told the Archbishop how one supplier had been berated for the poor quality of his bricks:

'Fain would he have excused himself, but his handie worke spoke against him, and we were so round with him, that he burste into tears, saying, he was never the like served in anie worke; he was ashamed of it, he could not excuse it, it was the wickedness and deceitfulnesse of the yearthe.'

At one point in the excavation of the foundations, Fynche reported:

'the laborers have digged up four skulls and the bones of deade persons in the trench that they are now digginge, next the highway leadinge to the Parke'.

This discovery drew no further comment from Fynche, his letter to Whitgift concluding with what he considered to be the most significant news:

'I thank God, our groundworke is greatlye commended of all that view the same. And I hope well that will like his Grace at his cominge; for it is not slubbered uppe [carelessly covered], *but strongely done.'*

The building was completed at a total cost of £2,716 11s.11d. Well over four hundred years later, and now a Grade 1 Listed building, it still stands in the centre of Croydon, and continues to offer the accommodation for elderly residents that Whitgift prescribed. Sadly, for twenty-first century inhabitants, the fields, orchard, vines and arbours, provided by Whitgift for his Hospital, have long since been built over; only the historical record, confirmed in Walter Godfrey's article, preserves the memory of the *'bowling alley'*, the *'walnutt tree garden'*, the *'apricocke'* trees, and the six hundred *'rose-sets'*, brought especially from Worcestershire to Croydon, in 1614.

Whitgift took the Audience Chamber and adjoining rooms in the Hospital for his own use, even though his Palace was only a quarter of a mile away, down the hill. Carefully drawn-up regulations set out the terms on which needy individuals could be admitted, both men and women, twenty-eight in total, and up to forty if funds were available. Men aged sixty and above, who had served in the Archbishop's household in Lambeth, or in Croydon, were to be given priority. Whitgift personally relaxed one of the orders, which barred married couples from admission, in order that *'Thomas Elthon of the parish of Croydon, Blynde and of the age of 71 years'* could enter *'with his aged wife'*. Close by, he established his School, following the example of Eastbridge, and also of his predecessor Grindal's school, at St Bees in Cumbria. Whitgift specified that the Headmaster, to be known as the Schoolmaster,

'shall have for his lodging and dwelling place…that howse which I have builded for that purpose, adjoining to the saide Hospitall, and nere unto the saide schoolehouse…and shall also have the some of twentye pounds yearly for his stipande…together with other further commodities of corne or wood'.

The first to hold the post was Ambrose Brygges, who was chosen by Whitgift; provision was made for all future Headmasters of the School to be directly appointed by the Archbishop, and his successors, a practice which has continued to the present at Whitgift

School. The addition of two further schools, Trinity, in the mid nineteenth century, and Old Palace in the late twentieth, and of two care homes, Whitgift House and Wilhelmina House, is testimony to the strength of an evolving Foundation; his Foundation's varied institutions, in the twenty-first century, reflect the scale and generosity of the original bequest of buildings and land that has sustained them. Paule praises his master's generous spirit, that reached much further than aiding his Foundation alone:

'he would be exceeding cheerful and affable with his own Gentlemen and servants (of whom Paule was one)*…he was very liberal in rewarding them, both with leases, offices, and otherwise with supplies, as their occasions required, out of his purse…As his Bounty was very great towards his own (for in that number likewise he always accounted the poor society of his Hospital) so were his hands every-where reached out to necessities of all sorts. Yea such was his charity, that if he had seen poor men…he would have given them money, and waste ground to employ in gardening, or some such use as might be for their relief. Or if he heard that any of his poor neighbours were decrepit, or destitute of means to follow their trade, he would supply their needs either with money or fewel, and sometimes poor watermens wants with boats, and such like'.*

Unsurprisingly, Whitgift made provision for his burial to be in Croydon, in the Church of St John the Baptist, now Croydon Minster, very close to his Palace. He was the second of five Archbishops to make this choice, Edward Grindal being the first, and subsequently William Wake, John Potter and Thomas Herring doing so. A charred inscription was all that was left of Grindal's memorial, after the fire of 1867, and the other tombs were lost; miraculously, Whitgift's survived intact. The scale of Whitgift's bequest to Croydon was immediately known and appreciated. John Rhodes, Minister of Enborne, in Berkshire, wrote in his Epitaph for the Archbishop, published in 1604:

'O carefull Croyden, now to thee I speake,
For thine and Lambeths losse, our harts will breake.
Ah! Who shall do as White-gift did for you?
Lay up and build Schoole and Almshouses too?
Lord I know none, such Blacke Swans are too rare.
Each man is bent to Avrice every where,
None but the Lord, can set such men in place,
Gladly to pitty the poore man and his case:
Let White-giftes worke, that stands thus in the eye,
On each Arch-Byshop for like worke still cry.'

(Above) The Audience Chamber, in Whitgift's Hospital of the Holy Trinity

(Left) The Armada Chest, probably made about the time of the famous sea battle, which for many years held the Whitgift Foundation's documents and precious items

(Opposite) Statue of John Whitgift on a plinth against the Old Town Hall, in Croydon

A PLEASANT

Comedie, called

Summers last will and
Testament.

Written by *Thomas Nash.*

Imprinted at London by *Simon Stafford,*
for *Water Burre.*
1600.

Thomas Nashe.

(Opposite) Thomas
Nashe's 'Summer's Last
Will and Testament',
performed in Croydon
in 1592, and published
in 1600

(Above) Thomas
Nashe, line engraving,
seventeenth century,
after an unknown
artist

(Left) The restored Church of St John the Baptist (now Croydon Minster), seen from a courtyard next to the fifteenth century chapel at what was Croydon Palace, Whitgift's residence when Archbishop; the Palace now forms part of Old Palace of John Whitgift School

(Below) The Great Hall of Whitgift's Palace, painted in the late nineteenth century, by FL Emanuel

(Left) A beechwood bowl, from which the brethren (residents) of the Hospital of the Holy Trinity drank. The inscription reads: 'What sirrah holde your peace thirst satisfied cease'

(Below) The original Schoolmaster's House, in a late nineteenth-century engraving

(Overleaf) Hospital of the Holy Trinity in the 1840s, from a later engraving by MJ Starling

7

Pro Ecclesia Dei (For the Church of God) – The End of an Era

During her last illness, in March 1603, Whitgift was one of the very few people that the Queen wished to have around her; Paule records that,

'*though by reason of her melancholy disease, she was impatient of others speeches with her, yet was she well pleased to hear the Archbishop, the then Bishops of London, and Chichester, and the now Bishop of Worcester, with some other Divines, give her comfort and counsel to prepare her self to God-ward*'.

John Hayward's sermon, preached at Paul's Cross on 27 March, the Sunday after the Queen's death, gives one of the earliest accounts of the circumstances, emphasizing how important Whitgift's presence was as a comfort to the Queen:

'*...on the Wednesday, death approaching...the right reverend father, the Lorde Archbishop comming in unto her at three in the after-noone, he put her in minde of the sufferings of Christ, the meanes of her salvation; of remission of sinnes and eternall life, and most gladly she harkened unto him, testifying her joy with her hand, which shee could not so well do with her voice. And when the reverend father, knowing how soone sicke parties are wearied, did withdrawe himself, giving signe with her hand, she called him unto her the second time. And when, againe after a second speech, hee withdrew himself, she beckned to have him come unto her the third time...*'

Did the Queen die in Whitgift's arms? Accounts of witnesses to her death have been shown to differ markedly as to who was present; the courtier, Thomas Ferrers, was one who reported that *'the L. Archbishope of Canterbury…was with her* [the Queen] *until the last gaspe'*. Whitgift walked, as a chief mourner, in the Queen's funeral procession, to Westminster Abbey, on 28 April.

The Archbishop outlived the Queen by less than a year. In his seventies, and still mentally sharp, he had become physically more suited to a quiet life, supervising his Croydon Hospital and School, than to the rigours of his job at the head of the Church. Already, three years earlier, on 7 June 1600, he had lamented to his friend, Matthew Hutton, Archbishop of York:

'I am here verie much troubled with the appeasing of newe controversies about praedestination, justification, liberum arbitrium [free will], *the state of the Fathers before the coming of Christe, inhaerent justice, and such like matters…*[take care] *least they say that zeale is quenched in you and that you doate in your old age, as it pleaseth some here to say of mee.'*

He depended increasingly on his friend, the Bishop of London, to be his understudy; it was therefore Bancroft who fulfilled the Archbishop's traditional duty, and rode out to meet King James, as he progressed south from Scotland to claim the English Throne. Whitgift mustered the physical strength to be present at two early proclamations of James as Elizabeth's rightful successor, one with members of the Privy Council at Whitehall, the other at Cheapside, with the Lord Mayor. He was also strong enough to be able to officiate at the Coronation, in July 1603. He put a brave face on his situation, writing to an old friend, the Earl of Shrewsbury, in December 1603, *'I thank God I go on as I was wont to do, altho at this present I am tainted with my old disease, the jaundice'*. He was increasingly unwell, and had become little more than a figurehead in the Church. Somehow, he managed to attend the Hampton Court Conference, in January 1604. Puritan ministers were sounding-out the new King, and his Bishops, and seeking a response to their so-called Millenary Petition, which had been handed to James as he travelled down from Scotland. They were testing how far the Elizabethan Settlement would hold in the new reign. Whitgift could take comfort from the fact that no points of significance were conceded by the King at the Conference, and the religious *status quo*, which Whitgift had worked so hard for two decades to champion, survived intact into the Stuart era.

The Hampton Court Conference was to prove Whitgift's last important engagement. Travelling in his barge across, or along, the Thames, to Fulham, Whitehall, or the near twenty miles from Lambeth to Hampton Court, in wintry weather, followed by a series of lengthy meetings, had taken a toll on his fragile health. He had caught a heavy cold, and, on 26 February, having again crossed in his barge to Whitehall, for a meeting, Whitgift collapsed, as the company was about to go in for dinner; he was paralysed down his right side with a stroke. He was taken back to Lambeth Palace, and clung on to life for three days. King James visited him, but Whitgift could barely speak. He died the next day, 29 February, in the evening. His last recorded words were *'Pro Ecclesia Dei, Pro Ecclesia Dei'*, (For the Church of God); they were uttered while King James was present, but it is unclear whether they were intended as an injunction to the King, or as a comment on Whitgift's own life, or both. The following evening, Whitgift's body was taken to Croydon, where it rested overnight in the Church of St John the Baptist. The parish register records:

'[Whitgift] *was buried the morninge followinge by two of the clocke in the chappell where his pore people doe usuallie sitte: his funeral was kepte at Croydon the 27th day of Marche followinge, anno dni. 1604.'*

At the funeral service in March, Whitgift's former students from Trinity College, Cambridge, were strongly represented. One, Gervase Babington, gave the sermon; Whitgift had recommended him to be Bishop of Llandaff in 1591, and Babington had subsequently been promoted, on his advice, to Whitgift's former Bishopric in Worcester. Two others, the Earl of Worcester and Lord Zouch, attended the hearse. Matthew Hutton, the Archbishop of York, a former Fellow of Trinity, and Whitgift's predecessor as Lady Margaret Professor of Divinity in Cambridge, wrote:

'Many may and do lament, that His Majesty hath lost a faithful, good counselor, the Church a great and notable pillar and patron, and myself also have special cause to sorrow for the want of such an ancient, constant and dear friend.'

Although Sir George Paule described the funeral as *'very honourably solemnized'*, the fierce controversies that punctuated Whitgift's life were reflected at his passing. Amongst the elegiac laments and epitaphs pinned to the Archbishop's hearse was a crude and hostile poem, entitled *'The Lamentation of Dickie for the Death of his Brother Jockie'*, Dickie being Bancroft, Whitgift's successor as Archbishop, and Jockie being Whitgift himself:

'Reformers hinderer, trew pastors slanderer,
The papists broker, the Atheists Cloker
… The dumb dogs patron, non resid[e]ns champion
A well a daye is dead & gone
…Papiste be sadd, Athiests runn madd
Grone formalists, mone pluralists
Frowne ye docters, mourne yee Procters
…Goe all daunce about his hearse,

& for his dirge chant this verse
Our great patron is dead and gone,
& Jhockey hath left dumb dickey alone.'

Alastair Bellany's article, 'A *Poem on the Archbishop's Hearse'*, published in the *Journal of British Studies*, describes how members of the Privy Council, and Robert Cecil in particular, led the campaign to identify and prosecute the author, a Puritan, Lewis Pickering, who was arraigned before the Judges of the Court of Star Chamber by Sir Edward Coke, the Attorney General. Coke, yet another erstwhile Trinity College student, was determined to defend the former Master's reputation. Pickering was found guilty, fined, sentenced to imprisonment and to being put in the pillory, in London, Croydon and Northampton; his ears were to be nailed to the pillory if he refused to confess to his crime. Bellany also cites Thomas Sackville, the Earl of Dorset, who sought the exercise of poetic justice; as Pickering had called for Whitgift's corpse to be placed in a Croydon collier's sack, Dorset wanted Pickering himself to '*weare a Collier's sacke upon the pillorie at Croydon'*. The strength of feeling in support of Whitgift's memory, and in favour of his successor, Bancroft, had found powerful expression.

Whitgift had other, happier memorials. A gentleman usher in his household expressed his personal sadness in a short poem, which begins:

'*Pure saints, by heaven refyn'd from earthlie drosse,*
You duelye can esteeme your new increase;
But our soules' eyes are dymme to see the loss,
Great prelate, wee sustaine by thy decease.'

Another epitaph described Whitgift as '*the lantern-light of England'*, now extinguished. It was composed by the octogenarian poet, Thomas Churchyard, whose muse was stated by Thomas Nashe, himself a beacon to younger writers, to be '*grandmother to our grandiloquentest poets at this present'*. Churchyard, who only outlived Whitgift by a few months in 1604, entitled his poem '*Churchyard's Good Will, Sad and heavy Verses, in the nature of an Epitaph, for the loss of the Archbishop of Canterbury'*:

'*The staff of stay, from feeble folk is gone,*
The lantern-light of England is burnt out,
The spectacle for world to look upon
The fickle wheel, of Fortune turned about.
…A Prelate great is taken from our State…

Whitgift his name, great gifts of God he had,
Won worthy fame, as white and black now shows,
His presence made, full many people glad,
Always got friends, and still reclaimed foes,
Held liberal house, and kept a Lordly train,
Fed rich and poor, with all God sent and gave,
Hoarded not up, nor loved no greedy gain,
Knew that all we, shall carry nought to grave,
But shrouding sheet, good name, and true renown
That wins from hence, an everlasting Crown.

Croydon can shew, his works, life, laud and all,
Croydon hath lost, the Saint of that sweet shrine,
Lambeth may cry, and Canterbury may call,
Long for the like, with woeful weeping eye...'

Whitgift's last will and testament had already started to take effect during his lifetime; he had lived to see the beginning of his principal and enduring legacy, his Foundation in Croydon. He left behind no great works of theology, unlike his contemporary, Richard Hooker, a minor clergyman but leading theologian, although a number of Whitgift's manuscripts remained unpublished at his death. Paule records that the French Ambassador in London enquired as to what books Whitgift had written that he might read, given the Archbishop's reputation as the preminent cleric of his day. On hearing that, although Whitgift had left material in defence of ecclesiastical government, his legacy was his Hospital and School in Croydon, the Ambassador declared: *'Truly an Hospital to sustain the poor, and a School to train up youth, are the worthiest books that an Archbishop could set forth.'* The first bequest in his will was a confirmation of Whitgift's love of music, the singing, the playing of organs, cornets and sacbuts, which he had enjoyed in church services, or in the *'shew'* he commissioned for the Queen in Croydon. He left to his successors as Archbishop

'...the organs remaining in the Chapels at Lambeth and Croydon and also the musical instrument in the Chamber at Lambeth called the Presence Chamber and the instrument of musick in the lobby or entrance into the same Chamber and all the pictures upon tables and the maps being in my gallery at Lambeth...'

Gifts were made to members of his family, his two surviving brothers, William and George, and to his nephews and nieces. Although, in his lifetime, Whitgift had already ensured that family members were well provided for with property, he wished to make some more personal gifts, just as his own father had left him a gown and silk doublet. His brother, William, was given one of his best horses and its harness, and the plate used for private dining at Lambeth Palace. Bridget, his youngest, and unmarried, niece, received £200 and fifty ounces of gilt plate. His nephew, John, his main heir, received property in Kent, and, again, more personal items: *'all such my implements household stuff furniture plate ready money books movables and utensils whatsoever as shall remain...in Shorne* (his principal house in Kent).'

Whitgift's other substantial bequest was that of his library. He had amassed one of the major libraries of his time, six thousand volumes of books and manuscripts. It was a main interest of his, and many additions to the list of books in the catalogue of the library are in Whitgift's own handwriting. Bibles and theological works are listed, amongst which are copies of a communion book in the Welsh language, reflecting his commitment to the publication of the Bible in Welsh, together with a very diverse range of volumes: Spanish and Italian grammars; classical authors, historical and literary works; books on travel and geography, atlases, maps, and one of the earliest books on angling; Camden's Britannia, Stow's Survey of London, Gerard's Great Herball, Ascham's Scolemaster, and Elyot's Governour. Works by Aristotle, Virgil, and Thucydides rubbed shoulders with those of Chaucer, Dante, Erasmus and Sir Thomas More – Whitgift possessed an autograph copy of More's poems for the Coronation of Henry VIII. He also chose to keep copies of several of the significant pamphlets from his campaign against the Puritan Marprelate tracts. He was continuing to add volumes to his library right up until his final illness. To his successor, Bancroft, his close friend and ally, he left *'all my written books in paper* (i.e. printed) *touching matters of learning or any waie concerning matters of the Churche'*; Bancroft utilised these, together with his own, to establish the Lambeth Palace Library, in his will, in 1610. Whitgift also gave Bancroft a more personal gift: *'for his paines to be taken in the executing of this my Will my best gold ringe at his choice.'* He bequeathed his manuscript collection to the Cambridge colleges with which he had had a close association. Trinity College took the finest, well over one hundred, having had first pick of *'such of my written parchment books as they have not alreadie',* followed by Peterhouse, with other, specific donations to Pembroke Hall. The manuscripts would have come principally from libraries destroyed at the time of the Dissolution, in the 1530s. A significant proportion is thought to have come from Christ Church, Canterbury, and St Augustine's, Canterbury, proving Cambridge to be Whitgift's academic spiritual home, the University profiting at the expense of his Diocese.

Whitgift initially fared well at the hands of historians; John Stow, who dedicated his *'Annales'* to the Archbishop, described him as *'a man born for the benefit of his country and the good of his church',* and William Camden declared that the Archbishop had *'devoutly consecrated both his whole life to God and his painful labours to the good of his church'.* Sir George Paule, in his eulogistic biography, published in 1612, praised Whitgift's principal achievement in maintaining the Church of England:

'happy surely was it for that crazy state of the church (for so it was at this Archbishop's first coming and a long time after) not to meet with too rough and boisterous a physician; for he preserved it with conserves, and electuaries, and some gentle purges, which with strong purgations in all likelihood might have been much more endangered'.

Indeed, Whitgift's success contrasts sharply with Archbishop Laud's subsequent failure. Laud, a successor in the reign of Charles I, could, with profit, have studied Whitgift's example, where an acceptance of at least superficial conformity sufficed to avoid deeper divisions. Laud's over-ambitious policies and misguided leadership inflamed opposition, provoked unneccessary divisions in the Church, and saw both King and Archbishop executed; Elizabeth and Whitgift died in their own beds.

However, over the more than four centuries that have passed since Whitgift's death, and despite the Church which he fought so hard to defend being still established, he has not lacked detractors, and he remains one of the most controversial of the Archbishops of Canterbury. The nineteenth-century historian, Thomas Babington Macaulay, himself a former student of Trinity College, Cambridge, twisted the knife with a famous denunciation, a description of Whitgift at the time when he was Master of the College:

'Whitgift, afterwards Archbishop of Canterbury, a narrow-minded, mean, and tyrannical priest, who gained power by servility and adulation…He was now in a chrysalis state, putting off the worm and putting on the dragon-fly, a kind of intermediate grub between sycophant and oppressor. He was indemnifying himself for the court which he found it expedient to pay to the Ministers by exercising much petty tyranny within his own college.'

It was a vicious, personal attack, very 'Martinist' in style, on the man who had hugely enhanced the reputation of Macaulay's College, and it coloured subsequent interpretation of Whitgift's life. It has lost much of its force now that Macaulay's own, pseudo-liberal creed has been debunked. Macaulay's deep-seated prejudices, to several of which Whitgift fell foul, and his sweeping, egotistical judgments, are themselves offensive to twenty-first century minds, an example being Macaulay's claim that his educational policies in India would do a great service by eradicating Hinduism within thirty years.

Whitgift rose high in Church and State above all because of his talent, allied with an exceptional work ethic, and attention to detail. In these respects, as a notable son of

Lincolnshire, he had not a little in common with Lincolnshire's most famous daughter, Margaret Thatcher, nearly four centuries later. Perhaps in contrast to Thatcher however, Whitgift also owed his success, in attaining his major goals, to his often surprising moderation, which enabled him to work with the Queen and the variety of opinions represented in government and on the Privy Council. Across a broad spectrum, from Catholics to moderate Puritans, he was rarely seen by his peers as extreme. Burghley could not have tolerated Whitgift, the Queen would not have appointed him to the Archbishopric, and he could not have retained the Earl of Essex as a friend, had he truly been an extremist. The Earl of Salisbury even declared that *there was nothing more to be feared in his government (especially towards the latter time) than his mildness and clemency*, and many called for much tougher action against recusants than Whitgift generally imposed.

With devout Puritans he shared many Calvinist beliefs, and, with Catholic contemporaries, a commitment to individual devotion. For Whitgift, however, the key ingredients in religious observance were attendance at a formal service, within an established, national Church, led by a well-educated minister who could utilise the power of a carefully-prepared sermon. Paule idealised Whitgift's talent in this regard:

'he would oftentimes preach so early in the morning in some parish-church, both in Worcester, and Canterbury, that he came afterwards to the sermon in the Cathedral Church. His gift that way was excellent, as if you had heard Saint Augustin himself, or some of the ancient Bishops in the Primitive Church. His gesture, and action in the pulpit, so grave and decent, his words coming from him so fatherly, and comely...[with] *substantial matter, full of good and sound learning, plentiful in authorities out of scripture, fathers and school-men'.*

Whitgift benefitted, in his own career, from the patronage of men such as Dr Perne and Bishop Cox, in a manner that was usual for his century, and helped others in a similar way: a whole string of Trinity College, Cambridge men, many of whom became Bishops in his Church; the poor scholars drawn to his *'little Academy'* in Lambeth Palace, who were found preferments and advanced in their careers; or particular individuals, such as the Welsh scholar, William Morgan, or his comptroller, George Paule. Whitgift significantly helped Morgan, whom he had known in Cambridge and Ely, in the publication of the first Welsh Bible, credited by Wynford Vaughan Thomas with playing a major part in saving the Welsh language. Whitgift continued to assist: in recommending Morgan to be Bishop of Llandaff, in the mid 1590s; in the publication of a revised translation of the Welsh Prayer Book, in 1599; and in supporting Morgan's subsequent appointment to the Bishopric of St Asaph, in 1601. Paule, Whitgift's loyal servant for two decades, was made Registrar for the Ely Diocese, and a seat in Parliament was found for him.

Whitgift showed himself, in his relations with Burghley, Elizabeth's chief minister, to be far from the servile creature portrayed by Macaulay, vigorously opposing Burghley on many occasions. Nor was he merely servile, as opposed to scrupulously loyal, to the Queen. He maintained his friendship with the Earl of Essex throughout the 1590s, in the face of royal displeasure; and a fascinating personal letter, from Whitgift to the Queen, survives, that shows he was not afraid to speak his mind, in attempting to dissuade her from any thoughts of following her father's example in despoiling the Church:

'I beseech your majesty to hear me with patience, and to believe me that yours and the church's safety are dearer to me than my life, but my conscience dearer than both; and therefore give me leave to do my duty, and to tell you that princes are deputed nursing-fathers of the Church, and owe it a protection; and therefore God forbid that you should be so much as passive in her ruins, when you may prevent it; or that I should behold it without horror and detestation, or should forbear to tell your majesty of the sin and danger of sacrilege.'

Collinson, the distinguished historian of Tudor Puritanism, dismissed Whitgift as a very limited man, with a schoolmasterly turn of mind, who was intolerant of any deviation from the rigid standards he set for the clergy. This assessment, less dramatic than Macaulay's, may be seen as equally unfair. Whitgift, a gifted man, was, on the contrary, capable of showing a remarkable understanding of the points of view of others. This is demonstrated in the following extracts from his letters, exceptional for his time:

'I find no one certain and perfect kind of government prescribed or commanded in the scriptures to the church of Christ...I condemn no churches that have appointed any order for the electing of their pastors which they think to be agreeable to their state, and most profitable for them... every church may do therein as it shall seem to be most expedient for the same. That may be profitable for the churches of Geneva and France, etc, which would be most hurtful to this church of England'.

'I confess that in a church collected together in one place, and at liberty, government is necessary... but that any kind of government is so necessary that without it the church cannot be saved, or that it may not be altered into some other kind thought to be more expedient, I utterly deny.'

Another more personal, yet equally-striking, example of the breadth of view of which he was capable can be found in the *'shew'* he commissioned for Elizabeth I's visit to his Croydon Palace in 1592. He allowed the author, Nashe, to poke fun at all that he most valued, in front of the Queen, his guests and his household servants.

In Croydon, Whitgift has long been appreciated for the immense, positive impact the legacy of his Foundation has had on the Town, and on many of its inhabitants, young and old. The development of his Hospital and School was the principal interest of his final years. The exceptional generosity with which they were established enabled them to prosper down the centuries. Dom. Aidan Bellinger and Stella Fletcher, in *The Mitre and the Crown*, their study of the Archbishops of Canterbury, describing Whitgift as the *'complete Elizabethan primate…fearless and…conscientious'* remark:

'Looking at the entire history of the Archbishops, it might be argued that the strength of Whitgift's posthumous association with Croydon runs a close second to the cult of Becket in Canterbury.'

Whitgift himself frequently lamented that he was misunderstood by contemporaries; the following heartfelt plea is contained in a letter sent to Burghley from Croydon on 15 July 1584, following questioning, by some on the Privy Council, of Whitgift's motives:

'It is strange, that a man of my place, dealing by so good warrant as I do, should be so encountered, and, for not yielding, be counted willful. But I must be content, Vincit qui patitur [he conquers who endures]. *There is a difference betwixt willfulness and constancy. I have taken upon me, by the place which I hold under her Majesty, the defence of the religion and the rites of the church of England, to appease the schisms and sects therein, to reduce all the Ministers thereof to uniformity, and to due obedience, and not to waver with every wind; which also my place, my person, my duty, the laws, her Majesty, and the goodness of the cause do require of me, and wherein the Lords of her Highness's most honourable Privy Council (all things considered) ought in duty to assist and countenance me.'*

His patient application and endurance, in the spirit of *vincit qui patitur*, the motto of his Foundation, had sustained him through all adversity, and upheld the Elizabethan Settlement. Despite his success, it seems that he may well have expected that the antipathy, and lack of understanding, that he had frequently encountered during his own lifetime, would continue after his death. The inscription chosen for his portrait in the Chapel of his Hospital of the Holy Trinity, the almshouses he founded in Croydon, with its last word *'INVIDIA'*, in capital letters, suggests as much, in stating:

'Feci quod potui, potui quod, Christe, dedisti.
Improba fac melius, si potes, INVIDIA.'

It translates as

'I did what I could, Christ, what you gave me to do.
Those ILL-DISPOSED towards me, do better if you can.'

(Opposite) Queen Elizabeth I, by an unknown artist, painted in the late sixteenth century

(Right, above) Letters Patent, signed by Queen Elizabeth I, dated 22 November 1595, authorising Whitgift to found the Almshouses

(Right, below) Detail from a stained glass window in Grimsby Minster, showing Whitgift praying at the death-bed of Queen Elizabeth I

JOHN WHITGIFT ABP CANTERBURY.

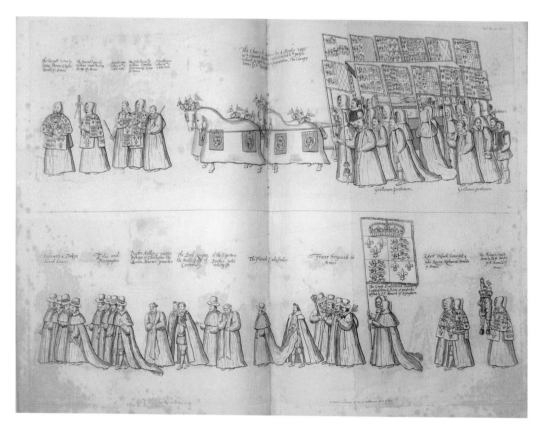

(Above) William Camden's drawing of the funeral procession of Queen Elizabeth I. Whitgift is the thirteenth figure from the left, on the bottom row

(Left) Shoes found on John Whitgift's memorial in Croydon Minster, and reputed to be those of the Archbishop

(Above) Portrait of
Archbishop Whitgift,
towards the end of
his life, now in Knole
House, by an unknown
artist

(Opposite) Whitgift's tomb in Croydon Minster

(Above) Statue of Whitgift, dating from 1871, holding his Almshouses in his left hand, which now stands in the Founder's Garden at Whitgift School, in Haling Park

(Left and below) Mazers, or drinking bowls: an inventory, from 1601, of the contents of the Armada Chest of Whitgift's Hospital, catalogues a 'mazer tipped with silver and gilt' as the gift of a Mr Boulton (left); another, recorded in an inventory of 1634, bears Whitgift's coat of arms (below)

*(Above) Portrait of
John Whitgift, by
an unknown artist,
from the Chapel at
his Hospital, bearing
the inscription ending
'INVIDIA'*

Select Bibliography

Anderson, J C	Monuments and Antiquities of Croydon Church	1856
Arber, E (Ed)	An Introductory Sketch to the Martin Marprelate Controversy 1588-1590	1895
Archer, J	The Progresses, Pageants and Entertainments of Queen Elizabeth I	2007
Ascham, R	The Scholemaster	1579
Ayre, Rev J	The Works of John Whitgift – 3 vols	1851
Baildon, W P	Les Reportes del Cases in Camera Stellata 1593–1609 – from the Original Ms of John Hawarde	1894
Barrow, H	The examinations of Henry Barrowe John Grenewood and John Penrie, before the high commissioners, and Lordes of the Counsel	1596
Beavis, J	The Croydon Races	1999
Bellany, A	A Poem on the Archbishop's Hearse: Puritanism, Libel, and Sedition after the Hampton Court Conference Journal of British Studies Vol 34 April	1995
Bellinger, Dom A, and Fletcher, S	The Mitre and the Crown	2005
Brook, VJK	Whitgift and the English Church	1957
Camden, W	Britannia	1586, 1607
Carley, J	In private men's hands – The Library of Archbishop John Whitgift John Coffin Memorial Palaeography Lecture	2010
Churchyard, T	Churchyard's Good Will	1604
Clare, J	Art made tongue-tied by authority – Elizabethan and Jacobean Censorship	1990
Clarke, M L	Classical Education in Britain, 1500-1900	1959
Clegg, C S	Press Censorship in Elizabethan England	2004
Collinson, P	The Elizabethan Puritan Movement	1967
Collinson, P	Richard Bancroft and Elizabethan Anti-Puritanism	2013
Colthorpe, M	Queen Elizabeth I and the Croydon Horse Race Surrey Archaeological Society vol 77	1986
Cressy, D	Book burning in Tudor and Stuart England in The Sixteenth Century Journal, Vol 36, No.2	2005
Dawley, P Mills	John Whitgift and the Reformation	1955
Dean, D	Law-Making and Society in Late Elizabethan England – The Parliament of England 1584-1601	1996
Degenhardt, J H and Williamson, E	Religion and Drama in Early Modern England – The Performance of Religion on the Renaissance Stage'	2011
D'Ewes, Sir S	The Journal of All the Parliaments During the Reign of Queen Elizabeth I	1682
Ducarel, Dr	Some Account of the Town, Church and Archiepiscopal Palace of Croydon	1783
Dyer, A D	The City of Worcester in the Sixteenth Century	1973
Ferrers, T	King James His Welcome to London	1604
Fleay, F G	Queen Elizabeth, Croydon, and the Drama Balham Antiquarian and Natural History Society	1898
Hammer, P	The Polarisation of Elizabethan Politics – The Political Career of Robert Devereux	1999
Hayward, J	God's Universal Right Proclaimed, A Sermon Preached at Paules Crosse	1604
Heal, F	Of Prelates and Princes – the Economic and Social Position of the Tudor Episcopate	1980
Gajda, A	The Earl of Essex and Late Elizabethan Political Culture	2012
Garrow, D W	The History and Antiquities of Croydon with a variety of other interesting matter	1818
Godfrey, W H	The Whitgift Hospital, Croydon Home Counties Magazine, January	1901
Greg, W W (Ed)	Henslowe's Diary 1591–1609	1908
Guy, J	The Reign of Elizabeth I – Court and Culture in the last decade	1995

Hobson, J M	The Book of the Wandle	1924
Hobson, J M	Some Early and Later Houses of Pity	1926
Jack, A (Ed)	As You Like It – Christopher Marlowe, William Shakespeare	2013
Jack, A (Ed)	Hamlet by Christopher Marlowe and William Shakespeare Vol II	2005
Lake, P	Moderate Puritans and the Elizabethan Church	2004
Loades, D M	Elizabeth I	2010
Loomis, C	The Death of Elizabeth I – Remembering and reconstructing the Virgin Queen	2010
Lyly, J	Pappe with an Hatchet	1589
McCullough	Sermons at Court – Politics and religion in Elizabethan and Jacobean preaching	1998
More, D A	Article in The Marlovian Newsletter	1996
Morgan, V	A History of the University of Cambridge, Vol 2 1546 – 1750	2004
Morrissey, M	Politics and the Paul's Cross Sermons, 1558-1642	2011
Nashe, T	Summer's Last Will and Testament	1600
Nicholl, C	A Cup of News – The Life of Thomas Nashe	1984
O'Sullivan, W	Archbishop Whitgift's Library Catalogue TLS 3 August	1956
Oswald, O	Old Palace, Croydon Country Life Magazine – April	1965
Paget, C G (Ed)	Abstracts of the Ancient Muniments of the Whitgift Foundation Croydon	1934
Paule, Sir G	The Life of John Whitgift	1612
Pearson, A F S	Thomas Cartwright and Elizabethan Puritanism	1925
Penry, J	A Treatise containing the Aequity of An Humble Supplication	1587
Penry, J	The Appellation of John Penry unto the High Court of Parliament	1589
Penry, J	To My Beloved Wife Helener Penry	1593
Percy, F H G	Whitgift School	1991
Percy, F H G	What Really Happened in Hamlet – Madness in Elsinore is Sanity in Southwark	2006
Pickering, L	The Lamentation of Dickie for the Death of his Brother Jockie	1604
Raine, J (Ed)	The Correspondence of Dr Matthew Hutton	1843
Raymond, J	Pamphlets and Pamphleteering in Early Modern Britain	2006
Rhodes, J	An Epitaph on the Death of the late Archbishop of Canterbury	1604
Rhodes James, M	The Western Manuscripts in the Library of Trinity College, Cambridge	2009
Riggs, D	The World of Christopher Marlowe	2004
Shuger, D	Censorship and Cultural Sensibility – The Regulation of Language in Tudor-Stuart England	2006
Simon, J	Education and Society in Tudor England	1966
Skeel, C A J	The Council in the Marches of Wales	1904
Stow, J	Survey of London	1603
Stow, J	The Annales of England	1601
Strype, J	The Life and Acts of John Whitgift – 3 vols	1822
Tatton-Brown, T	Lambeth Palace – A History of the Archbishops of Canterbury and their Houses	2000
Trevelyan, G M	Trinity College An Historical Sketch	1983
Upton, J (Ed)	Spenser's Fairy Queen, new edition	1758
Walton, I	The works of Richard Hooker – 3 vols	1845
White, E M	The Welsh Bible	2007
Whitgift, Archbishop J	A Godlie Sermon preched before the Queen's Majestie at Greenwich 26 March 1574	1574
Whitgift, Archbishop J	A most godly and learned sermon, preached at Pauls crosse the 17 of November 1583	1583
Williams, Penry	The Council in the Marches of Wales under Elizabeth I	1958

John Whitgift's legacy: the Whitgift Foundation, in the twenty-first century, comprises, from the top left:

Old Palace of John Whitgift School

Whitgift's Hospital, his Foundation's Almshouses

Whitgift School

Wilhelmina House

Whitgift House

Trinity School

(Opposite) Bronze statue of John Whitgift by Sam Holland, in the grounds of Whitgift School

JOHN WHITGIFT

The Author

Dr Christopher Barnett was an Exhibitioner at Oriel College, Oxford, where he gained an MA and a DPhil in Modern History. He also held a Bible Clerkship, as John Whitgift did at Trinity College, Cambridge. He was appointed, by Archbishop Robert Runcie, to be the twenty-sixth Headmaster of Whitgift, the School founded by Archbishop Whitgift in Croydon, a post he has held for nearly a quarter of a century. In 2009, he wrote and directed *Hidden Treasures from the Mary Rose*, an acclaimed exhibition displaying many of the finest artefacts recovered from Henry VIII's warship, the *Mary Rose*. In 2016, he will be directing another major exhibition, *Remembering 1916: Life on the Western Front*.